The Soccer Referee's Manual

Third edition

The Soccer Referee's Manual

David Ager

CONTEMPORARY BOOKS

Library of Congress Cataloging-in-Publication Data

Ager, David.
    The soccer referee's manual / David Ager.—3rd ed.
       p. cm.
    Includes index.
    ISBN 0-8092-9735-3
    1. Soccer—Refereeing—Handbooks, manuals, etc. 2. Soccer—Rules
  —Handbooks, manuals, etc. I. Title.

  GV943.9.R43 A54 2001
  796.334'3—dc21   00-42908

Laws of the Game reproduced with the authorization of Fédération Internationale de Football Association

Cover photography courtesy of Allsport, London

First published in 2000 in the United Kingdom by A&C Black (Publishers) Ltd
35 Bedford Row, London WC1R 4JH

This edition first published in 2001 in the United States by Contemporary Books
A division of NTC/Contemporary Publishing Group, Inc.
4255 West Touhy Avenue, Lincolnwood (Chicago), Illinois 60712-1975 U.S.A.
Printed and bound in Great Britain
International Standard Book Number: 0-8092-9735-3

00 01 02 03 04 05   18 17 16 15 14 13 12 11 10 9 8 7 6 5 4 3 2 1

Contents

Preface to the Third Edition vii
Foreword viii
Introduction ix

Unit 1 The referee, assistant referees and linesmen 1
    Part 1 • Law 5 – The referee 1
    Part 2 • Law 6 – Assistant referees 13
    The Cooper Test of physical fitness 25

Unit 2 Laws 1–4 26
    Part 1 • Law 1 – The field of play 26
    Part 2 • Law 2 – The ball 33
    Part 3 • Law 3 – Number of players 35
    Part 4 • Law 4 – The players' equipment 38

Unit 3 Laws 7–11 42
    Part 1 • Law 7 – The duration of play 42
    Part 2 • Law 8 – The start of play 43
    Part 3 • Law 9 – Ball in and out of play 45
    Part 4 • Law 10 – Method of scoring 47
    Part 5 • Law 11 – Offside 47

Unit 4 Fouls and misconduct 58
    Part 1 • The penal offences 58
    Part 2 • Non-penal offences 65
    Part 3 • Other offences 70
    Part 4 • Dealing with misconduct 72

Unit 5 Free kicks and penalty kicks 85
    Part 1 • Free kicks 85
    Part 2 • Penalty kicks 91

Unit 6 The throw-in, goal kick and corner kick 102
      Part 1 • The throw-in 102
      Part 2 • The goal kick 106
      Part 3 • The corner kick 107

Laws of the Game 110

Assessment 135
Notes on Diet and Fitness 143
Useful addresses 149
Index 150

Preface

The Soccer Referee's Manual is a very useful book for those wishing to develop their understanding of The Laws of the Game.

The author, David Ager, is an experienced and well respected referee instructor. I have followed his work carefully since he became a Football Association Licensed Referee Instructor.

His book has been carefully researched and revised regularly to keep up to date with Law changes introduced by the International FA Board.

The book explains the Laws in simple, accessible language and illustrations are used well to supplement the text. The questions that appear at regular intervals invite the reader to check out his or her knowledge. You might find it interesting to tackle the questions before you read each chapter. You may then be surprised to find you have more to learn than you thought.

For would-be referees and those in the early years of their refereeing career, there is plenty of advice on how to develop techniques that will improve their performance.

I hope you enjoy reading the book. If it inspires you to become a referee so much the better. Your County Football Association will be delighted to welcome you.

John P. Baker, May 2000
Head of Refereeing
The Football Association

Foreword

The Soccer Referee's Manual is an in-depth study of the Laws of the Game, and it is particularly suited to candidates of the FA referees course, with its emphasis not only on the Laws, but also on their practical application.

The role of the referee has become more onerous in the past few years, and in evaluating his duties, tasks and responsibilities, this book will also provide interest to all who enjoy this great game, including players, managers, coaches and the media. The manual contains many illustrated examples, along with test questions aimed at assisting the trainee referee, and testing the knowledge of more experienced officials.

David Ager is a most respected Cornwall County FA referee and FA Licensed Referee Instructor. Now into its second edition, his manual will prove an excellent resource for referees at all levels of the game, and for anyone interested in soccer.

Martin Bodenham
National List referee
Former FIFA referee

Introduction

Association football, or soccer, was developed in the nineteenth century as a game for public schoolboys in an attempt to develop character, instil teamwork and provide an outlet for youthful high spirits. From these roots it has become one of the world's leading sports, played by millions of people. From being a sport purely for young men, soccer is now being played increasingly by women and older men.

Although the game is primarily about participating, it is impossible for competitive soccer to be played without referees. As society has become more and more competitive, so soccer has become more concerned with winning. This has not only led to the referee becoming a more important figure in the game, but it has also placed referees under much greater pressure.

The main aim of this book is to prepare candidates for the FA Class 3 Referee's Certificate. This is the starting point for a career in refereeing. By working through the manual, the reader can gain an understanding of the laws of the game, and their application in practice.

A second aim is to help the practising referee to refine and develop his game, and to revise his knowledge and understanding of the laws. The material will encourage referees to give some thought as to how they approach the game, and the techniques used to apply the laws.

The third aim is to provide players, spectators, enthusiasts and the media with an opportunity to gain an understanding of the laws of soccer, and the job of the referee. As the decisions of referees become increasingly important, and the subject of continuing controversy and argument, an awareness of the refereeing role becomes more valuable to anyone with a love of the game.

For the sake of brevity and clarity, the manual is written using the male gender throughout. The author wishes to make it clear that this is in no way intended as a slight against women's involvement in soccer generally, or in refereeing in particular. Just as increasing numbers of women are now playing the game, so more women are taking up refereeing, a trend that is greatly welcomed.

Note Other than those given in the Cooper Test of physical fitness, all measurements are in imperial units.

The author

David Ager, a former player and club official, originally qualified as a referee in 1975. In 1987 he became a Football Association Licensed Instructor of Referees. In his resident county of Cornwall he has been involved in the training of new referees and in the training of already qualified officials. He is also a Football Association Registered Assessor of Referees, and advises on referee promotion for Cornwall County Football Association.

David enjoys all aspects of the game, both at professional and amateur level, and is a supporter of Ipswich Town, his origins being in East Anglia. He is married with two grown-up children.

UNIT 1
The referee, assistant referees and linesmen

PART 1 • Law 5 – The referee

At first it may seem strange that the Law relating to referees is tucked away in fifth place. However, it is not so strange when we consider that in the early years of soccer there was no mention of referees in the Laws of the Game at all. The reason for this was simple – there were no referees! Any dispute was dealt with by a discussion between the two captains, and for most decisions the players were assumed to be honest and sporting so that no disagreement would occur which could not be resolved in this sporting way. As soccer became more popular and more competitive in the late nineteenth century, the need for an independent referee became essential.

The enlarged role of the referee thus necessitated a clear definition of his powers. These are found in Law 5, with Law 6 devoted to the assistant referees.

Law 5 is broken down into 18 parts, each defining either a duty that the referee must perform, or a power that he may use where necessary in the game.

(i) Enforce the Laws
The referee has a duty to enforce the Laws. Quite simply, that is the prime reason for him being there. The referee is expected to uphold and interpret the Laws of the Game in order to ensure that a fair, sensible and competitive game of soccer takes place.

(ii) Control the match in co-operation with the assistant referees and, where applicable, with the fourth official
The role of the assistant referees is considered in detail later in this unit, as is that of the fourth official. It is, of course, essential that there is a good level of understanding between the referee and his two assistants so that the game can be controlled efficiently and competently. The fourth, or reserve, official is normally only available in senior professional soccer.

(iii) Ensure that the ball meets the requirements of Law 2

This is considered in more detail in another unit, but for now it is worth remembering that you are responsible for ensuring that the ball provided by the club is acceptable. A well organised club will provide this before the start of the game – if you are unlucky, it is presented to you, covered in mud, at the centre spot as you are about to spin the coin, and it is often at the wrong pressure. The referee should try, if at all possible, to get hold of the ball well before the start of the game.

(iv) Ensure that the players' equipment meets the requirements of Law 4

This is dealt with in Unit 2. Suffice to say that the Laws require players to wear shinpads for their own safety in addition to the normal equipment of jersey, shorts, socks and boots. It is also essential that players' equipment is safe so that other players are not exposed to risk of injury during the course of the game.

(v) Act as timekeeper and keep a record of the game

It is important that the referee keeps a clear record of the game. To do this, referees have a match card, an example of which is illustrated below.

Fig. I Example of a clean match record card

COMPETITION						DATE:	
TEAMS	H			A		CAPTAIN'S Nos. H A	
COLOURS			K.O.		K.O.		
GOALS	1st		SCORE		SCORE		
	2nd						
		NAME/ No.	CODE	NAME/ No.	CODE		
CAUTIONS AND DISMISSALS							
SUBSTITUTES						ASSISTANTS	
						H	
						A	

Perhaps the most important feature of the card is the score. Given the physical and mental pressure he is under, it is easy for the referee to lose count of the score in the game, and a careful record will ensure that this error is not made. With the card, there is a space for writing in the half-time scores so that if an entry is made in the wrong place in the second half, it can be discovered more easily. Some referees write the half-time score down in words as well as numbers in order to make errors less likely. The importance of this cannot be underestimated as the score that the referee enters on the submitted result card will be accepted without question by the authority under whom the game is being played. If an error is made in this respect, the referee will be placed in a very embarrassing position.

It is also important to write down clearly the time of kick-off. A good tip here is to indicate the time the game is due to end as well. This gives an extra check on when the referee will need to signal for the end of the half, and saves some mental arithmetic during the match, when he will have more important things to think about.

Normally, the FA will require the *full* name of the culprit if anyone has been cautioned or dismissed, so the referee should make sure that he has this information. It is also useful to put the time of the offence down. This helps the referee to distinguish between incidents in a game, and is also required by the FA in the report. Below is a completed match record card, which illustrates the points made.

Fig. 2 Example of a completed match record card

COMPETITION	South Western Counties League					DATE: 31/11/97	
TEAMS	H	Redruth	A	Porthtowan		CAPTAIN'S Nos. H 7 A 5	
COLOURS		Red	K.O. 2.30	Blue	K.O. 3.30		
GOALS	1st	I I I (Three)	SCORE 3	I (Four)	SCORE 4		
	2nd	I (One)	I	I I (Three)	3		
		NAME/ No.	CODE	NAME/ No.	CODE		
CAUTIONS AND DISMISSALS		Paul BARKER (10) 2.35	Dissent	Ned BLAKLEY (3) 3.05	Foul Play		
		Bruce TAYLOR (6) 2.45	Un-Sp Beh	Peter GRENFELL (2) 3.40	Dissent		
SUBSTITUTES		Peter WALTERS ✓		Ken KEEMER			
		Chris COOMBES		Jeff PREECE ✓			
		Barry CUDMORE ✓		Simon MARTIN		ASSISTANTS	
		Robin TUCKER		Tony BILSLAND		H Liz ASHTON	
		Graham EMMETT		Mike TRENERRY		A Alan PEARLE	

(vi) Stop, suspend or terminate the match for any infringement of the Laws

(vii) Stop, suspend or terminate the match because of outside interference of any kind

Here the referee is empowered to stop the game for free kicks, etc. as required, a power that is, perhaps, fairly obvious. If spectators get out of control, or the light fades, or the weather makes the game impossible to complete sensibly or in safety, then the referee should abandon it. If he does this, it is important to report the matter to the appropriate authority (either the league concerned or the FA, depending under whose auspices the game is being played). They, and they alone, have the power to determine whether the game should be replayed or whether the score at the time of abandonment should stand. An important point to remember is that once the referee has made his decision to abandon the game, he should *not* allow himself to be talked into changing his mind. This can create problems. If, for example, a hailstorm descends, he can temporarily stop the game and delay a decision as to whether to continue, but should not be talked into returning once he has made up his mind to abandon the game and has communicated his decision to the two teams.

(viii) Stop the match if, in his opinion, a player is seriously injured and ensure that he is removed from the field of play

(ix) Allow play to continue until the ball is out of play if a player is, in his opinion, only slightly injured

The referee should stop the game if a player appears to be badly hurt. If a player is only slightly injured, then he can be dealt with *off* the field of play. Making a judgement here can be difficult for the referee. The best advice is, if in doubt, stop the game and don't move the player. This is especially important if the player has sustained a head injury. Although television has, in recent years, highlighted the play-acting of some players in the professional game, this is very rare in junior soccer.

When a player goes down injured, it is usually best to give him the benefit of the doubt and delay the game. The referee should not be talked into trying to move the player if he judges it unwise. The players will be looking to the referee to take sensible decisions, so he should err on the side of caution and take no risks. If possible referees should try to take some First Aid training.

A few years ago, I refereed an evening game in which the home goalkeeper seriously injured his knee in a collision. We kept him warm and comfortable, and, despite the gathering gloom, delayed the re-start of the game until an ambulance had arrived. When it did, the medics took 15 minutes to pick the player up and put him into the ambulance, vindicating my decision not to attempt to inexpertly move him off the field, despite pressure from several players who wanted him moved to the touch-line so that the game could continue.

(x) Ensure that any player bleeding from a wound leaves the field of play. The player may only return on receiving a signal from the referee, who must be satisfied that the bleeding has stopped
Recent concerns over the dangers of contracting diseases through contact with blood from an infected person has caused FIFA to require referees to follow this procedure.

(xi) Allow play to continue when the team against which an offence has been committed will benefit from such an advantage
It is often the case that although an infringement has occurred, the award of a free kick would be to the advantage of the offending team. A simple example is that of a player who breaks through the defence and although fouled by an opponent, retains his footing to have a good chance on goal. A free kick in this situation would allow the defence to re-group, and thus gain them a considerable advantage. The referee needs to make up his mind whether to give a free kick or to play the advantage. Until the 1996/7 season, once the referee had decided to play the advantage, it was impossible for him to change his mind and give the free kick if the advantage did not work out, for example where the player loses his footing following a foul tackle. The Law now allows the referee to pull back the play for the free kick if the advantage does not work out. This decision must be taken within a few seconds. It is not possible for a free kick to be awarded after the fouled player, having regained his balance, has miskicked a shot on goal, or played a poor pass to a colleague.

Perhaps the best advice to a new referee is not to worry too much about the advantage clause until you are more confident about its use. It is better to give a few too many unnecessary free kicks than to see the game go out of control because you are trying too hard to play the advantage. Also, there are some circumstances in which applying the advantage clause may not be advisable. For example, if a really serious foul or an assault has taken place the game should normally be stopped immediately, so that the player(s) concerned can be dealt with.

Although it is possible to caution or send off a player when the game stops later on, failure to do so quickly may result in an ugly situation turning into an impossible one, with players taking the law into their own hands and a brawl developing.

Another situation where the advantage clause should be treated with respect is if the offence has occurred in or near the penalty area of the non-offending team. It is very tempting, and often very sensible, to allow play to continue without a free kick where, following an offside or a foul on a defender, the goalkeeper has the ball in his hands and can clear it quickly upfield. The referee should, however, treat this with some caution if there is any risk of the defender failing to control a ball coming towards him, in which case the advantage gained by the attacking side will be considerable. Another danger is if the goalkeeper has been unfairly challenged but retains the ball. He may prefer to take a few seconds to recover before playing on, and a free kick would be welcome here. If there is a danger of further confrontation between the players following the original challenge, then this also should be taken into account and a free kick awarded.

It is important to remember that advantage is *not* the same as possession. Just because a player has maintained possession of the ball does not mean he gains an advantage from playing on.

Finally, it is very important for the referee to remember to clearly inform the players that he is applying the advantage clause. He should extend both arms forwards, and shout 'Play on! – Advantage!', so that the players know that he has acknowledged an infringement and is playing the advantage. Failure to do this will mean they assume that he has missed the offence, and they will begin to lose confidence in him.

(xii) Punish the more serious offence when a player commits more than one offence at a time

This is dealt with more fully in Unit 4, and represents a straightforward, commonsense approach. A simple example to illustrate this: if a player impedes the progress of an opponent, an offence that is normally punished by an indirect free kick, but before the referee has blown his whistle to stop play the same player pulls his opponent back, a direct free kick should be awarded to penalise the second, more serious offence.

(xiii) Take disciplinary action against players guilty of cautionable and sending off offences. He is not obliged to take this action immediately but must do so when the ball next goes out of play

Cautions and sendings off are dealt with fully in a later unit, but for now it is worth remembering that the referee has the power to caution or send off players where appropriate from the time he arrives at the ground. This means that he can quite legitimately caution a player *before* the game has actually started. Another point worth remembering is that any referee who is in charge of a game played between

FA registered teams has this power. If, therefore, a club official takes over in the absence of an official referee, he too can caution or send off players.

(xiv) Take action against team officials who fail to conduct themselves in a responsible manner. The referee may, at his discretion, expel them from the field of play and its immediate surrounds
Though this is dealt with fully in Unit 4, it is worth noting that the referee has full jurisdiction over club officials and may take action against them if they misbehave.

(xv) Act on the advice of assistant referees regarding incidents that he has not seen
This is dealt with later in this unit. Where the assistant referee is a qualified, and neutral, referee, as you would find in senior soccer, he would be relied upon to provide advice to the referee on all incidents where his view was better than that of the referee.

(xvi) Ensure that no unauthorised persons enter the field of play
Here the referee is given the powers to stop anyone else from entering the field of play. This is very important. If a player is injured, then it may be necessary for the trainer to come on the field to attend to him. It is not necessary for an entourage of trainer, manager, substitute and a couple of supporters to come on as well. If there is some controversy in the incident that led to the player being injured, then the arrival of these unwanted people may result in a confrontation that he may find hard to control. As with so much in refereeing, prevention is better than cure, so the referee should be firm and *only* allow on to the field those who *have* to be there.

It is now possible for coaching from the side lines to occur, provided the coaching takes place in the 'technical area'. This means the area immediately around the team bench. Referees should beware of allowing coaching to be undertaken elsewhere, as it may distract opponents unfairly.

(xvii) Re-start the match after it has been stopped
To make it clear that you wish the game to re-start, it is necessary to signal this to the players. This does not necessarily mean blowing the whistle; you could simply shout to the players to continue. For many stoppages, it is best to encourage the game to continue to flow, so for throw-ins and goal kicks, or minor infringements, there is little need for any signal. If, however, the game has been stopped for a reasonable period of time, then it is best to use the whistle to make it clear

that you are re-starting after a break. I will look at aspects of this later in the course, when we consider free kicks and other re-starts.

(xviii) Provide the appropriate authorities with a match report that includes information on any disciplinary action taken against players and/or team officials and any other incidents that occurred before, during or after the match

The handling of disciplinary matters is dealt with fully in Unit 4. It is clearly essential that where the referee takes disciplinary action, this is properly reported to the authority under whose auspices the game is being played.

Some other points are worth noting. The first is that it is important to realise that the referee, once having re-started the game, cannot reverse his decision. If the game has not re-started he *can* do so, for example in the light of advice from an assistant referee. An example of this is when a goal has been scored, but the referee cancels his decision to give a free kick for offside to the opposing side following consultation with his assistant.

Another point to remember is that referees should be distinctive in dress from the players. This is normally no great problem since, you would think, no team is likely to arrive dressed in black, which is the normal colour for referees in junior soccer. In fact, about the third game I refereed involved a college team that arrived on the field wearing black shirts. I walked over to an adjacent field to seek advice from a more experienced referee: 'That's all right', he said cheerfully, 'just collect your fee and go home. You can't referee them.' I wandered over to the team to tell them that I couldn't referee an all-black team. 'That's OK', said the captain, 'they're reversible.' Sure enough, the players took off the shirts and turned them inside out to reveal a pale blue colour. It is worth remembering, of course, that occasionally teams do play in dark blue when the referee agrees to wear a different colour.

To win the respect of players and spectators, the referee should:

1 learn and understand every Law
2 be absolutely fair and impartial in every decision
3 keep physically fit and in good training.

Although this book should give you a good understanding of the Laws of the Game, referees must make every effort to keep up-to-date, and they must refresh their knowledge. This can be done by joining the local branch of the Referees' Association, where problems and the application of the Laws are discussed. Failure to understand the Laws of the Game leads to the charge of inconsistency and reduces the standing of referees, and it will also impede the progress of the individual in his refereeing career.

Being absolutely fair and impartial may appear to be obvious, but can, at times, be a little difficult to achieve. Where the referee has had more pressure put on him from one team, it may be that he begins to weaken, and gives that team more '50-50' decisions than he should. Some teams will try to 'soften up' the referee by continually questioning or commenting on his decisions, and the referee should be aware of this before he loses his impartiality.

Another problem may occur if a referee feels that a decision in the early part of the game to give a penalty, for example, was unfair, and he then tries to make up for this later in the match. This is disastrous, wins him no friends and will ensure that he loses control of the game. If he has made a bad decision, it is something he will just have to live with. If it's any consolation, referees at all levels will admit to making bad decisions now and again.

I am always amazed at the poor physical condition of a minority of referees. A lack of mobility is by no means uncommon in local parks as an unfit official attempts desperately to keep up with play. If the referee is reaching an advanced age, this may be understandable, but when he is in his twenties or thirties it is less forgivable. See the chapter 'Notes on Diet and Fitness', which gives essential guidelines for referees. Regular physical training, consisting of road running or cardio-vascular circuits, interval training and participation in sports such as squash and badminton, are important to good refereeing. Squash is especially valuable with its emphasis on swift physical and mental responses. If you are physically fit, you are more likely to be mentally alert and this is essential to successful refereeing. English FA National List officials (those who referee at the highest level) must complete the 'Cooper Test' satisfactorily, and this is reprinted at the end of this unit.

Now – before continuing – answer the following questions, without flicking through to check the text!

Unit 1

Questions

(Check your answers in the text.)

Q **1a** Can the referee caution or send off a player before the start of play?

Q **1b** Under what circumstances should the referee stop the game?

Q **1c** What can the referee do when he has applied the advantage clause but no advantage occurs?

Q **1d** If the referee plays the advantage and play then continues for several more minutes, can he caution or send off the offending player when the ball eventually goes out of play?

Q **1e** Can the referee reverse his decision?

Q **1f** What should the referee do in order to win the respect of players and spectators?

Q **1g** Under what circumstances should the referee allow people other than players and assistant referees on the field of play?

Q **1h** What can happen to a referee who fails to report misconduct that came to his notice?

Q **1i** Must the referee blow his whistle to signal the re-start of play?

The referee's equipment

It is essential that the referee arrives at the ground in good time, properly equipped. Failure to bring an essential piece of equipment, such as boots, or tunic, will present him with huge problems that, at best, will put him at a considerable disadvantage from the start, and at worst may stop him from refereeing the game altogether. Furthermore, he should ensure that his equipment is well cared for and appropriate to the task in hand.

Tunic, shorts and socks
The referee should make sure that these are clean and, if necessary, pressed. Socks should be washed after each game or those with white tops or hoops tend to turn grey. They are inexpensive and should be replaced as soon as this happens. It is certainly not acceptable for a referee to turn up in dirty, mud-stained shirt and shorts.

Flags

I am always amazed at the way some referees unthinkingly hand a dirty, dishevelled flag to their assistant referee at the start of the game. How can a referee command respect from an assistant referee if he offers him a mud-encrusted flag? It is very easy for the referee to wash his flags after a game and, if necessary, iron them before use.

Footwear

Needless to say, my earlier comments on clothing also apply to boots. These should be clean and polished. If white laces are worn, these should also be clean.

Whistle

The referee should ideally have two whistles, one spare in case the other fails. It is a good idea to have them on a lanyard – just a simple length of crêpe bandage is fine – so that the whistle is easy to hand. A word of warning here – don't run with the whistle in your mouth. If the ball is unexpectedly kicked at your face, you may suffer quite serious injury to your teeth.

Spare handkerchief

The referee will need a handkerchief for his own use, but a spare one could be invaluable too. This must be clean and unused, and is needed in case a player suffers from a cut or nosebleed and needs something to stem the flow or to protect the wound until more thorough first aid is available.

Watches

The referee should have two watches – one, at least, should be a stopwatch. Several good quartz wrist-watches are now available which have this facility, and a few have been designed purely for soccer timing. Beware of some electronic stopwatches: highly sensitive switches mean that these are often accidentally changed while in the referee's pocket or hanging round his neck.

Red and yellow cards

The use of red and yellow cards has become necessary at all levels of the game. These are usually made of plastic, and come in different shapes – one oval and the other rectangular. This avoids the embarrassment caused by the referee pulling out the wrong card by mistake. Some referees also try to avoid errors by keeping the cards in separate pockets.

A number of other items may be taken to a match. Of course, it is important to take a **coin**, and even more important to remember to take it out onto the field of play! Often, referees take an **adaptor** and a **bicycle pump**. Many less organised junior sides may lack these basic essentials; having them available may retrieve an otherwise impossible situation. Never underestimate the ability of clubs to be disorganised and badly equipped! This leads me to another item worth taking – toilet paper. A few years ago I was an assistant referee in a local cup final. The dressing rooms were full of players, club officials, match and league officials. A visit to the toilet, however, revealed a complete lack of paper!

Questions

(Answers on page 24.)

Q 1.1 What action could the referee take if he found that an assistant referee was unreliable and inefficient, or biased?

Q 1.2 During a match, a team disagree with the referee's decision and walks off in protest. After several minutes, the players cool down and express a wish to re-start the game. Should the referee now re-start?

Q 1.3 The referee is struck by the ball, which temporarily stuns him. The ball rebounds and enters the goal. Should the goal be allowed to stand, even though he couldn't see it?

Q 1.4 Just as the referee is about to start a game, he notices a player who is under suspension. Should he refuse to allow him to play?

PART 2 • Law 6 – Assistant referees

The referee should have two people to assist him, one on each touch line. Traditionally, these were known as 'linesmen', but recently they have been re-named 'assistant referees'. In a local game, they are generally connected with the clubs concerned, often being the trainer or substitute. Here they are now referred to as 'club assistant referees'. In more senior games they are qualified referees in their own right. Previously known as 'neutral linesmen', they are now just known as 'assistant referees'. To improve clarity, I will, where appropriate, distinguish between 'neutral' assistant referees and 'club' assistant referees. This reflects the fact that the former have a more responsible role in helping the referee to control the game.

According to Law 6, assistant referees are required to do the following: (1) Indicate when the ball has gone out of play for a corner kick, goal kick or throw-in. (2) Indicate which side is entitled to the corner kick, goal kick or throw-in. (3) Indicate when a player may be penalised for being in an offside position. (4) Indicate when a substitution is requested. (5) Indicate when misconduct or any other incident that is out of the view of the referee has occurred. This may be necessary when: a) the assistant is closer to the action than the referee; b) during a penalty kick – to see if the goalkeeper moves forwards before the ball has been kicked, and if the ball has crossed the goal line to judge if a goal has been scored.

The assistant may also be asked to enter the field of play in order to control the 10-yard distance law that opponents must observe when a free kick is taken.

In practice, it may be difficult for a club assistant referee to signal for misconduct without adequate training. Here the assistant may be asked to only signal for ball out of play and offside.

Many referees argue that running the line is a much more difficult job than refereeing. In addition to looking for the ball going out of play, an assistant referee must be aware of the possibility of a player being offside when the ball is kicked forwards. In signalling for a foul, an assistant referee may have to take into account the manner in which the referee is handling the game. Is he likely to prefer to play advantage, for example? Another problem is that an assistant referee is far nearer than the referee to any abuse or 'constructive criticism' on offer from supporters. Finally, while being cautious of abusing the referee, often players seem to regard the assistant referee as an easy target.

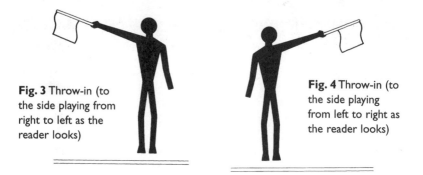

Fig. 3 Throw-in (to the side playing from right to left as the reader looks)

Fig. 4 Throw-in (to the side playing from left to right as the reader looks)

So, running the line well is far from easy. For a match to be well controlled, the referee and his two assistants need to work in close co-operation. Let us start, however, by looking at the signals that the assistant referees give to the referee. Firstly, there is the signal for a throw-in (fig. 3). The assistant referee points the flag clearly in the direction of play of the side that is entitled to the throw.

Note that in fig. 4 the assistant referee has put the flag in his left hand. This is important because if he holds the flag in his right hand he will cover part of his face and obscure his view of the game. There is also a danger that the signal will be less clear and even ambiguous.

The assistant referee should also give an indication for goal kicks. This can be seen in fig. 5, in which the flag is clearly pointed across the field to the goal area.

The final signal for the ball going out of play is the award of a corner kick. Here the assistant referee should point the flag to the corner quadrant nearer to them as shown in fig. 6.

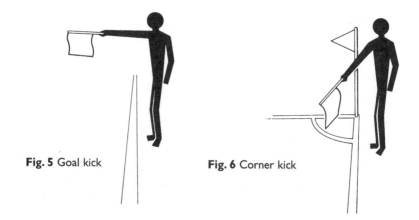

Fig. 5 Goal kick

Fig. 6 Corner kick

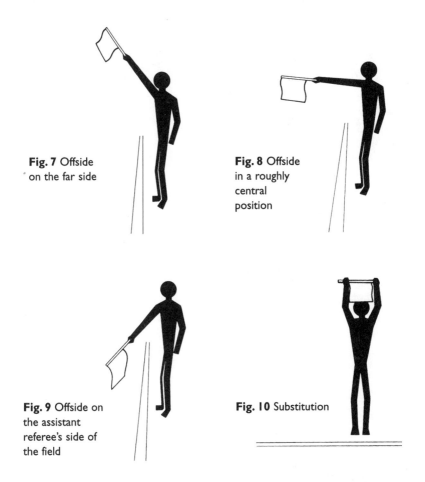

Fig. 7 Offside on the far side

Fig. 8 Offside in a roughly central position

Fig. 9 Offside on the assistant referee's side of the field

Fig. 10 Substitution

It is very important that the flag should be pointed to the *nearer* corner quadrant, and not the far one or this could be very confusing, with the referee unable to tell whether the signal being given by his assistant is for a goal kick, offside or a corner kick.

The signals for offside are quite simple. The assistant referee raises the flag with a flourish and, when seen by the referee, shows it as above.

In fig. 7, he is indicating that offside has occurred on the far side of the field of play. In fig. 8, the offside is roughly central. In fig. 9, the offside has occurred on the assistant referee's side of the field. We will consider this in more detail when we study the offside Law.

There is one more signal mentioned in the Laws. This is the signal for a substitution. Here the assistant referee simply raises his flag as shown in fig. 10, indicating that a team wishes to make a substitution. Note that this signal should never be given while the ball is in play, only when the game has stopped for some reason.

Two other signals used by assistant referees are not mentioned in the Laws. The first of these is where the flag is placed across his chest as shown in fig. 11, indicating that he is advising the referee that he should award a penalty kick.

Finally, the assistant referee may be asked to draw his arm horizontally across his chest to indicate that on his watch the period of play has been completed (fig. 12).

Fig. 11 Advising the award of a penalty kick

Fig. 12 Indicating that on his watch the 45 minutes of the half are completed

Questions

(Answers on page 24.)

Q 1.5 What colour should assistant referees' flags be?

Q 1.6 An attack takes place in which the ball is kicked into the goal, but after initially signalling a goal, the referee sees that the assistant referee's flag is raised. He goes over to the assistant referee who tells him that a player was in an offside position, interfering with play, and that the goal should not be awarded. What should the referee do?

Q 1.7 A neutral assistant referee sees a player assault an opponent, and draws the referee's attention to this. Unfortunately the referee has not seen the incident. What should the referee do?

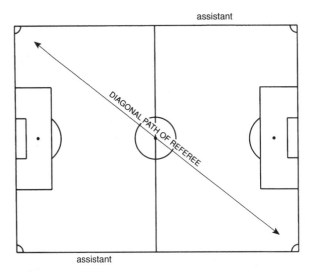

assistant

assistant

Fig. 13 The diagonal system of control

The diagonal system of control

Until the 1930s, assistant referees simply ran the length of the field, while the referee ran in an oval path around the field. In 1934, Sir Stanley Rous, later to become President of FIFA, introduced the diagonal system of control in the FA Cup Final between Manchester City and Portsmouth, which he refereed. This is shown in fig. 13.

The aim of this system is to achieve the greatest possible co-operation between the referee and his assistants, and the most efficient use of the three officials. If play is in one half of the field, the referee and one of his assistants will be able to cover it. Note that when this happens, the referee – if he is in a good position – will be able to see not only the action of the game, but also the signals of the assistants (for example, for offside or the ball going out of play, or for an offence committed in a position where the referee cannot see it clearly himself). The other assistant referee, meanwhile, has a good view of the other half, so that he can follow a quick breakaway if the ball is cleared upfield. The referee can choose to run either diagonal, incidentally, and many have a personal preference. His choice will be determined by factors such as wind, sun, slope of the field, or other factors.

Assistant referees

For the system to work well, there has to be a clear understanding between the referee and his assistants before the start of the game. Normally, the assistant referees will report to the referee before the start of the game to receive instructions from him as to how he intends to run the game.

In local, junior level soccer, and even sometimes in semi-professional matches, the referee must rely entirely on club assistant referees. Only in important games, such as cup finals, will the referee at this level have qualified referees to act as his assistants.

Club assistant referees are frequently officials of the team, often the manager or secretary, or sometimes one of the substitutes. Needless to say, quality varies considerably. The best often take their job very seriously, and are dedicated and honest. Sometimes leagues offer a trophy to the best assistant referee of the season, based on marks given by the referee. All too frequently, however, the club assistant referee has been forced into doing a job he would far rather avoid. The result is that his commitment to the task is lacking.

Neutral assistant referees, being referees who have been appointed to run the line, have wider responsibilities than those provided by the club, and the referee can come to depend on them for more support and advice. Anyone coming afresh into refereeing is unlikely to have the luxury of assistant referees for quite some time, but they are likely to find themselves acting in the role of assistant fairly soon.

If, for example in a junior game, neither team provides an assistant, the referee would be better to run a straight line – parallel to the touch lines and off centre – than a diagonal path. This involves less distance to run without any disadvantage in terms of match control.

Briefing the assistant referees

(A) Club assistant referees
Before the game, the referee should explain what he wants from his assistants. If he judges that an assistant referee has little interest, or is very inexperienced, this conversation can be trimmed down a little. I believe that an assistant who only gives signals for the ball out of play, for example, is better than nothing. If this is all he is able, or willing, to offer, I will accept it. It is important to show the club assistant referee that his involvement is appreciated and valued.

Instructions to club assistant referees should include the following:

1　The diagonal which the referee is going to run, thus determining the position of his assistants.
2　The forwards which the assistant referees are going to 'adopt'. In other words, whether they are going to judge offside against their own or the opposition forwards. (Often referees have a local convention about which to do.)
3　To indicate when the ball has gone out of play and to indicate which team is entitled to the throw-in, or whether to award a corner kick or goal kick.
4　Check that the ball is correctly placed in the goal area for the taking of a goal kick.
5　Stand near to the corner flag post and indicate if the ball goes out of play at the taking of a corner kick.
6　Signal to indicate if a player is in an offside position when the ball is played.

The club assistant referees should also be told that the referee must take the final decision. A good referee, however, will always acknowledge a signal from his assistant, even though he may wish to ignore or overrule it.

(B) Neutral assistant referees

Here, the situation is more complicated. The referee can rely far more on neutral assistant referees than he can on club assistant referees, and his instructions should be more wide-ranging and precise.

Instructions to assistant referees should thus include the following:

1　Who the senior assistant is. The senior assistant will have to take over if the referee is injured, and he thus must take note, not only of goals scored, kick-off times, etc., but also any cautions or dismissals that have been dealt with by the referee.
2　The time. The referee and his assistants should establish the time so that all their watches are synchronised.
3　Timing the game. Referees often ask the two assistants to give signals to indicate that there are just a few minutes left, or that the normal period of time is complete. Often, the referee will ask the more senior assistant to stop his watch for injuries or other stoppages (in line with the referee), while the junior assistant will be told to simply let his watch run through the full 45 minutes.
4　The side of the field that each assistant referee will take in each half, and the diagonal that the referee will be adopting. Normally, the senior assistant will be put on the side on which the dugouts are placed, so that he can handle substitutions during the game.

5 The assistant referees' duties prior to the start of the game. Usually, the referee will ask his assistants to inspect the goals before the start of the game to make sure that the nets are secure and that everything is safe and in good order.

6 Position to be taken at re-starts. The referee will usually say where he wishes them to stand at the taking of corner kicks, penalty kicks or goal kicks.

7 Signals. The referee may ask for certain signals from his assistants to indicate, for example, that the ball is in the correct position for a goal kick or corner kick.

8 Throw-ins. The referee will tell his assistants whether he wishes them to look for infringements with the feet or the hands at a throw-in.

9 Offside. The referee will explain what he requires of the assistant referees here. Often he will say 'The offsides are yours at all times', meaning that they should always keep in position to judge offside and he will accept their signals. Occasionally the referee will ask them to stand on the goal line at the taking of a free kick awarded to the attacking side near to the opposition goal. This is so that the assistant can judge the ball going over the line, or infringements in the goal area. In this case, the referee will judge offside when the kick is taken.

10 Penalties. The neutral assistant must watch for two things at the taking of a penalty kick. First, to see that the goalkeeper does not come off his line until the ball is kicked, and secondly, that the whole of the ball crosses the line for a goal.

11 Free kicks. The assistant may be asked to come on to the field of play to ensure that opponents are at least 10 yards from the ball. This is likely when a free kick to the attacking side is awarded close to the defending team's goal line and off the referee's diagonal.

12 Misconduct. The referee will ask the assistants to keep an eye on the game for any infringements by players. Normally this is only in the quarter (or sometimes half) of the field nearest to them. In particular, if an incident occurs off the ball that the referee does not see but an assistant does, then the assistant must inform the referee as soon as possible. If, as a result, the referee cautions or sends off a player, then the assistant who saw the incident must submit a misconduct report.

Positioning at re-starts

Much discussion is given up at Referees' Association meetings concerning the best position to take up at re-starts in the game. A good referee should be flexible about his positioning, since different games may require slightly different positions to be adopted. The following are straightforward suggestions that will illustrate some of the factors that the referee needs to consider.

Goal kicks

Here the referee takes up a position of 90° to the 'dropping zone', i.e. where he expects the ball to arrive. This is so that he can see fouls either by defenders pushing or attackers 'backing in' to opponents. It is important to remember that the dropping zone will vary from game to game according to wind strength, the overall length of the field, and the ability of players to kick the ball. The assistant referees should be in position to judge offside, but it is important to remember that players cannot be offside direct from a goal kick.

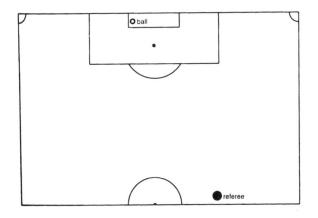

Fig. 14 Position of referee at goal kicks

Corner kicks

(A) On the referee's diagonal
In fig. 15 the referee has placed himself in a position midway between the outer corner of the penalty area and the outer corner of the goal area. In this position he has a good view of the penalty area and in par-

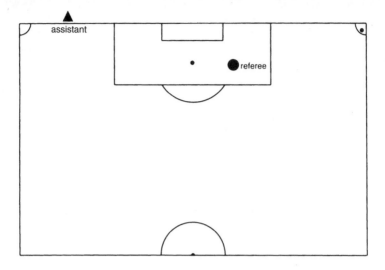

Fig. 15 Position of officials at corner kicks: on the referee's diagonal

ticular of the area in front of goal where incidents are most likely to occur. If the ball comes over the goal area, he can quickly move forwards to get a better view, while if the ball is cleared quickly upfield, he can make ground to cover a breakaway attack. Note that the assistant referee is standing a few yards from the corner flag post, along the goal line. He will be looking to see if the ball goes out of play. If he is a neutral assistant referee, he will be looking for any infringements as the ball is kicked.

(B) Off the referee's diagonal
Here the referee takes up a similar position. However, the assistant referee stands behind the corner flag post. This makes it easier for him to judge whether the ball has gone out of play from an outswinging corner that has then come back into play.

Penalty kicks
Here the referee stands in a position where he can best judge 'encroachment' by players. This is where a player enters the penalty area or comes within 10 yards of the ball before it is kicked. He can also see any misconduct by the kicker, and ensure that the player nominated to take the kick actually takes it. The assistant referee judges whether or not a goal is scored, and also whether the goalkeeper moves off his line before the kick is taken. Normally this responsibility would not be given to a club assistant referee. Positioning at penalty kicks is considered in more detail in Unit 5.

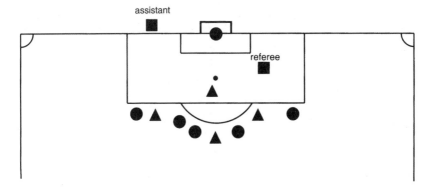

Fig. 16 Position of officials at penalty kicks

The fourth official

In professional soccer at the highest level it has become common to appoint a 'fourth official'. This was initially to provide cover in case of injury to the referee or one of his assistants during the game. Gradually this role has become more substantial.

Essentially his job is to control and record the substitutions, taking account of the players coming on to the field, and to take charge of the technical area in which the substitutes and club officials must stay. He is also expected to advise the spectators of how much 'stoppage time' there has been, and how much time needs to be added to complete the half.

The Laws were amended in season 2000/1 to allow the fourth official to provide more assistance to the referee. If, for example, the referee cautions the wrong player by mistake, or if a player who is cautioned has already been cautioned earlier in the game and is not sent off, the fourth offical can advise the referee of the error. He can also draw the referee's attention to or report any violent conduct that takes place out of the view of the referee and his assistants.

Finally, it is important to remember the old adage: 'you only get one chance to make a first impression'. When the referee walks out on to the field of play it is important he appears smart, confident and in control, to ensure he wins the confidence and respect of the players.

Unit 1

Answers

A 1.1 He is quite entitled to dispense with the assistant referee's services if he is dissatisfied with him. He should beware, however, because in a junior game it may be that he is the only person available. In this situation he may only wish to get rid of him as a last resort.

A 1.2 This is a situation in which he needs to use his common sense. If the team has walked off for several minutes, he would be wise to abandon the game. If he has already stated or threatened that he will end the game unless the team returns immediately, he would be foolish to continue. He should remember to send a report regarding the incident to the appropriate authority.

A 1.3 Unless he has a neutral assistant referee who has seen the incident clearly, he should not award a goal that he has not clearly seen. He must re-start play with a dropped ball when he has recovered. If he has been knocked out for more than a very brief time, he would be well advised not to continue the game, and if necessary to seek medical advice.

A 1.4 He cannot really refuse him permission to play. The referee is there to referee a soccer match, not to decide on the eligibility of players to play. It would be sensible, however, to warn the club secretary concerned that you are aware that he is under suspension, and also check to see if the player's name has been correctly entered on the team sheet that the referee signs at the end of the game. If it has, the appropriate authority will doubtless pick this up and take action. If his name is not there, you should refuse to sign the sheet and write to the governing authority explaining why.

A 1.5 Flags should ideally be bright, vivid colours such as red and yellow.

A 1.6 Provided the referee has not re-started the game, he can change his decision. If he is happy with the advice of his assistant, he may give an indirect free kick for offside. The referee, however, always has the final word and is ultimately responsible.

A 1.7 In this case, the referee should send the offending player off for the offence. Because he himself has not seen the incident, the referee cannot submit a detailed misconduct report, but must rely on the neutral assistant referee to do this.

Unit 1

The Cooper Test of physical fitness

(1) Repetition speed test

Referees are required to sprint a distance of 25 metres within 5 seconds, and to repeat this **eight** times with a 25-second rest between each run. The referee returns to the starting line during the 25-second rest period after each 25-metre run. Total test time = (5 seconds + 25 seconds) x 8 = 240 seconds (4 minutes).

A 15-minute recovery/rest period is allowed before the second test.

(2) Endurance test

The number of metres run on level ground in 12 minutes will be recorded, but anything less than 2600 metres will be considered a failure. Candidates must run for the full 12 minutes, and *not* stop when reaching the minimum distance, which applies irrespective of age.

Other minimum levels of performance that you *should* be able to achieve are: 400-metre run, 75 seconds; 50-metre run, 8 seconds; shuttle run 4 x 10 metres, 11.5 seconds.

The following table will give you some idea of your performance in relation to your fitness. (All values are the number of metres run over level ground for the duration of 12 minutes.)

Age	18–29	30–39	40–49	50–59
Very poor	–1750	–1500	–1250	–1000
Poor	1760–2240	1510–1990	1250–1740	1010–1490
In condition	2250–2750	2000–2550	1750–2250	1500–2000
Excellent	2760–	2510–	2260–	2010–

UNIT 2
Laws 1–3

PART 1 • Law 1 – The field of play

Law 1 is concerned with the field of play. Originally, before the Laws of the Game were properly set out in the middle of the nineteenth century, soccer was played on an area that might vary greatly according to the local geography. The need to standardise the Laws so that different teams could play with some certainty as to what to expect, led to a set of laws that determined the overall size and shape of the playing area, along with the internal areas such as the goal and penalty areas, and the goals themselves. These are all contained in this Law.

The external dimensions of a soccer field allow for some leeway, so that they can be adjusted to local conditions. In an international game, the degree to which the dimensions can vary is much more restricted to ensure a greater conformity.

Questions

(Answers on page 39.)

Q 2.1 What is the maximum and minimum length of a soccer field?

Q 2.2 What is the maximum and minimum width of a soccer field?

Q 2.3 What shape should the field of play *always* be?

As you can see, the field can vary greatly in its overall dimensions. Clubs can legitimately use this to their own advantage. Some years ago, Bolton Wanderers, a leading English club, deliberately narrowed their playing area by 10 yards when playing at home to Preston North End. In those days, Tom Finney, an England international, was playing on the wing for Preston, and he liked to play as wide as possible. The narrow field cramped his style and gave Bolton an advantage that was within the Laws.

In most situations, it is unlikely that a club will have marked out a playing area that is too big, although I have known clubs to switch a game to a boy's pitch that has been too small. If a referee suspects that a playing area is too big, he should report it so that it can be checked. If the area is too small, he should refuse to play a competitive game. However, it is possible to play veterans matches (i.e. players over 35 years old) on playing areas that are smaller than those required by the Laws.

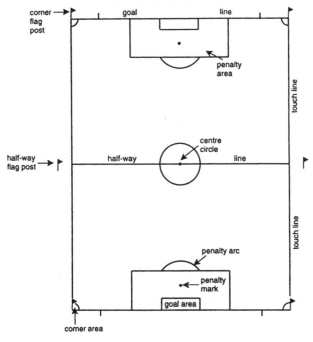
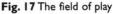

Fig. 17 The field of play

The markings

The overall marking of the field of play should be clear and distinctive, and in lines that are not rutted. Ruts can be dangerous if players catch their ankles in them, and also tend to 'trap' the ball so that it runs along the rut where it would otherwise have clearly gone out of play. Obviously the lines should be distinctive, otherwise the decision as to whether the ball has gone out of play becomes a matter for guesswork. Sometimes the lines become indistinct, due either to bad weather or, more frequently, the club not having bothered to re-mark the field after the previous week's game. If necessary, and if practicable, ask the club to re-mark where required so that mistakes are less likely to occur. Getting to the ground in good time will make this easier for the referee to deal with.

At each corner of the field there must be a corner flag, mounted on a vertical post. Each post should stand at least 5 feet above the ground, and have a non-pointed top. The reason for this is simple: if a tall player falls on to a post that is less than 5 feet it is likely to hit him in the chest, possibly injuring his ribs.

Half-way flag posts may be placed on the half-way line, and at least a yard outside the touch line, but these are not compulsory.

The centre circle

In the centre of the field a mark is made for the kick-off, or 'place kick'. From this mark a circle is drawn with a radius of 10 yards, known as the 'centre circle'. The purpose of this is to enable the referee to ensure that the opposing team are standing at least 10 yards from the ball at the kick-off.

The goal area

The goal area, or '6-yard box', is produced by measuring 6 yards from the inside of each goal post along the goal line, and from that point marking a 6-yard line into the field of play at right angles to the goal line. These lines are then connected by a line parallel to the goal line. The purpose of the goal area is twofold:

1 To show where a goal kick should be taken from.
2 To show where a free kick should be taken from when awarded for an offence which occurred within the goal area.

The penalty area

The penalty area is produced by measuring 18 yards from the inside of the goal posts, and then marking a line 18 yards into the field of play on each side of the goal. The purpose of the penalty area is threefold:

1 To define the area within which the defending goalkeeper may handle the ball, given certain restrictions explained later.
2 To show the area outside which the ball must be kicked to be in play following a goal kick or a defending team's free kick taken within the penalty area.
3 To show where, if one of the ten penal offences is committed by a defending player against an opponent while the ball is in play, the referee should award a penalty kick.

I will return to some of the points raised by this later in the manual. Remember that the penalty area *includes* the lines that border it, so that offences committed *on* the line are said to be committed *within* the penalty area.

Within the penalty area is a mark known as the 'penalty mark'. This is placed 12 yards from the goal line from a point midway between the goal posts, and indicates the point from which a penalty kick should be taken. Experience shows that this mark is likely to be wrong or missing or indistinct in a high proportion of cases. On one occasion, I refereed a local cup semi-final. On arriving at the ground, I inspected the field of play and discovered that one penalty spot was 14 and not 12 yards from the goal line. With plenty of time to spare, I was able to rectify this. A year later I was appointed to another cup semi-final on the same ground, and as I spoke to the assistant referees while we walked around the pitch before the start of play, I told them of the previous year's incident. As we looked at one of the penalty areas, sure enough the same mistake had been made again! Fortunately, I had a long surveyor's tape with me and we were able to check the dimensions. It doesn't take too much imagination to realise the problems a referee would face in a critical game during which the penalty spot has to be re-positioned before the kick can be taken.

Finally, an arc of radius 10 yards is produced from the penalty mark. This is to show the minimum distance from the ball from which all players must be when a penalty kick is taken.

The corner area

The other marking on the field that the Law requires is the corner area. Here a small quarter-circle of radius 1 yard is drawn from the corner flag post, and this simply shows the area within which the ball must be placed when a corner kick is to be taken. A mark may be made off the field of play, 10 yards from the arc, and at right angles to the goal line, to help check that defenders do not encroach within 10 yards of the ball at the taking of a corner kick.

Unit 2

Questions

(Answers on page 39.)

Q **2.4** Study the map of the field of play in fig. 18 and fill in the correct dimensions below.

(a) A–B .... (h) D–R ....
(b) A–D .... (i) S–T ....
(c) E–F .... (j) G–H ....
(d) E–N .... (k) P–X ....
(e) H–I .... (l) L–M ....
(f) G–P .... (m) L–W ....
(g) K–J ....

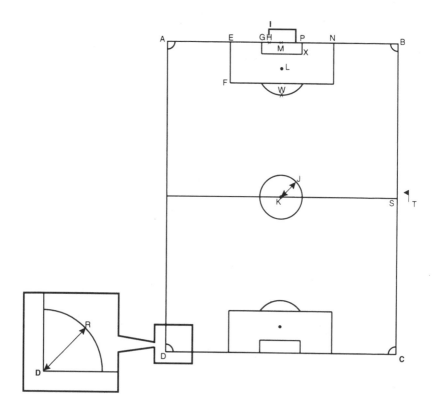

Fig. 18 Fill in the correct dimensions

Unit 2

Questions

(Answers on page 39.)

Q **2.5** The goal and touch lines are considered not to be part of the field of play. True or false?

Q **2.6** When measuring along the goal line to mark out the 6- and 18-yard lines for the goal and penalty areas, from which point should the measurement be taken?

Q **2.7** What is the minimum height of a corner flag above the ground?

Q **2.8** What is the minimum width of a touch line?

Q **2.9** What is the maximum width of a touch line?

Q **2.10** Would you allow a game on a field of play with dimensions of 100 yards by 50 yards wide?

Q **2.11** Is a penalty area of smaller size than stated in the Laws acceptable?

Q **2.12** On a playing area of minimum width, how far will the edge of the penalty area be from the touch line?

Q **2.13** On a playing area of maximum width, how far will the edge of the penalty area be from the touch line?

The goals

We turn now to a crucial piece of equipment. The problem with the goal, and particularly the goal nets, is that any defect can result in an otherwise legitimate goal being disallowed, or alternatively, an illegal one being given. So it is essential that the referee checks the goals very thoroughly for any weaknesses before the start of the game.

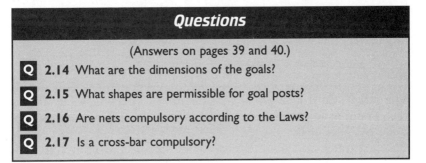

Questions

(Answers on pages 39 and 40.)

Q **2.14** What are the dimensions of the goals?

Q **2.15** What shapes are permissible for goal posts?

Q **2.16** Are nets compulsory according to the Laws?

Q **2.17** Is a cross-bar compulsory?

31

When the referee checks the nets prior to the game, he is looking for several things. The best way to show this is with an illustration (fig. 19).

1 The net is properly pegged down at the sides and behind the goal, so that the ball cannot squeeze under it either into or out of the goal.

2 The net doesn't sag and thus hinder the goalkeeper, and there are no large holes in the net through which the ball can pass.

3 The net is properly attached to the cross-bar and goal posts so that the ball cannot enter the goal through the side netting and the players cannot be impeded.

4 The posts are upright and firm, so that the goal cannot rock backwards and forwards.

5 The posts and cross-bar are painted white.

6 The goal line is clearly and accurately marked by a line that is as wide as the goal posts, so that the referee has a good view if and when a goal is scored.

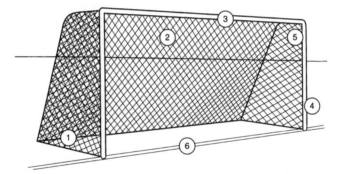

Fig. 19 What to look out for when checking goals

By now you may know that nets are not compulsory so far as the *Laws* of soccer are concerned, but almost all league and cup competitions now require nets to be provided as part of the *rules* of the competition. When you inspect the goals, ask the club to put right any defects that you have found before the kick-off.

Safety

The referee must give prime consideration to players' safety where the condition of the playing surface is concerned. Of course, sometimes the pitch may be severely ice-bound or rutted, or covered with standing water, and will thus clearly not only be dangerous but quite impossible to play on. Between a field in such a condition and a normal playing surface is a grey area in which the referee must use his judgement in making a decision as to whether a game should start or not. Rutted and frozen ground can be highly dangerous, as can a ground where a drain has failed, leading to a small bog appearing in one part of the field through which it is difficult to move. It may be possible to visit a ground well before the game and make an early decision, thus stopping the away team from having to undertake a long and pointless journey. Sometimes a locally based referee will do this if the ground is some distance from where you live, although some leagues may insist that the match referee makes every effort to inspect the field of play himself.

PART 2 • Law 2 – The ball

This Law is quite simple and straightforward, but there are some important tips and useful advice that the referee will need. It is vital that a ball used in a match is of standard specification, and the Law states what this specification is. Start by answering the following question.

Question

(Answer on page 40.)

Q 2.18 What are the five criteria to which a ball must conform to be acceptable?

Most balls used are made to standard weight and size, so this rarely causes a problem. But there are some training balls available of less than the regulation weight. As a ball ages, its shape can become deformed, and a referee may find himself being offered such a ball for a game, which he should, of course, reject. The most common problem occurs with the pressure of the ball. Often, club secretaries will either pump it up like a cannon ball, or alternatively, it will be too soft. With a poorly organised junior club, it is possible for the ball only to be given to the referee at the kick-off, with the result that the game must be delayed if it then needs to be inflated or deflated. Often, clubs fail to have the proper equipment to do this, which creates further problems.

A good tip here is to make sure that the ball is inspected well before the game starts. If possible, any spare balls which may be needed if the match ball is kicked out of the ground should also be checked. After this, the referee should also make sure that he retains possession of it. Most importantly, don't forget to take it out on to the field with you!

Another piece of good advice is to take along a bicycle pump and some valve adaptors. This will enable you to put things right quickly if the ball pressure needs to be changed. Remember that the Laws allow for the pressure to vary considerably.

Questions

(Answers on page 40.)

Q **2.19** A player shoots towards goal and the ball hits the cross-bar. As it does so, it bursts. What should the referee do and how should he re-start the game?

Q **2.20** You arrive at a ground to discover that there are only three corner flag posts, and two of these are only 4 feet 6 inches high. The club tells you that they have no other corner flag posts available. What should you do?

Q **2.21** You inspect a ground before the kick-off on a very cold afternoon, finding that it is very hard and frosty. Although mostly flat and even, some ruts exist where a tractor has been driven on what was a muddy patch on the edge of the field by the half-way line, and this seems dangerous to you. The two teams are keen to play, and tell you that they will be happy to accept full responsibility for any injuries that occur if the game is played. What action should you take?

Q **2.22** You are advised to get to the ground in good time to check the field of play. How early do you think the referee should arrive at the ground?

PART 3 • Law 3 – Number of players

This Law begins by stating simply that a team will normally consist of 11 players, one of whom shall be the goalkeeper. The Laws state that a match may not start if either team has less than seven players.

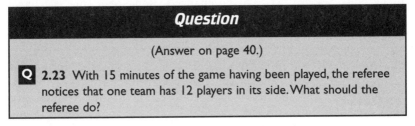

Question

(Answer on page 40.)

Q **2.23** With 15 minutes of the game having been played, the referee notices that one team has 12 players in its side. What should the referee do?

Goalkeepers

The goalkeeper has special privileges in his own penalty area, and the person acting as goalkeeper must be clearly identified by wearing a jersey which distinguishes him from both the referee, assistant referees and other players. The goalkeeper may change places with an outfield player provided this takes place:

• during a stoppage in the match
• with the permission of the referee.

Occasionally, but fortunately not very often, the goalkeeper may change places with another player *without* the referee's permission. When this happens, the referee should caution both players when the ball next goes out of play.

Coaching from the line

It is possible for club coaches to give tactical instructions, or to *coach* from the line. He must, however, return to his position within the technical area immediately after giving these instructions. The coach and other officials must remain in the confines of the technical area. They must also behave in a professional manner.

Unit 2

Question

(Answer on page 40.)

Q **2.24** A goalkeeper changes place with a defender without having obtained the permission of the referee. He removes the goalkeeper's jersey but stops the ball with his hand inside the penalty area, with the defender's shirt partly on. The defender has put on the goalkeeper's jersey. What should the referee do?

Substitutes

In virtually every competition, substitutes are permitted. In normal games the substituted player can play no further part in the match. A change in the Laws for season 2000/1 relaxed this for matches involving players under the age of 16, women, and veteran teams (over 35 years). The use of 'flying substitutions' is now allowed, subject to the agreement of the national associaton.

In friendly matches any number of substitutions may be used, provided that both teams concerned have reached an agreement on a maximum number and that the referee has been duly informed before the start of play.

Question

(Answer on page 40.)

Q **2.25** What is the maximum number of substitutions allowed in a competitive game?

The procedure for making a substitution is shown opposite. Note that the names of substitutes must be given to the referee before the start of play.

Unit 2

Making a substitution

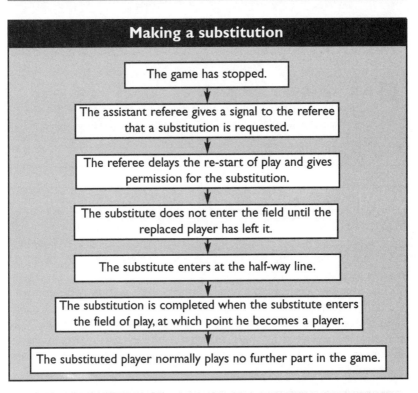

The game has stopped.

↓

The assistant referee gives a signal to the referee that a substitution is requested.

↓

The referee delays the re-start of play and gives permission for the substitution.

↓

The substitute does not enter the field until the replaced player has left it.

↓

The substitute enters at the half-way line.

↓

The substitution is completed when the substitute enters the field of play, at which point he becomes a player.

↓

The substituted player normally plays no further part in the game.

Questions

(Answers on page 41.)

Q **2.26** During a stoppage in play, a team wishes to make a substitution. As the substitute is about to enter the field, but before he does so, the substituted player uses offensive language to the referee. Should the referee allow the substitution to take place?

Q **2.27** In the second half of a match, and just after a goal has been scored, the referee realises that the scorer is a substitute who had come on at the start of the second half without his permission. What action should the referee take?

Finally, if a referee is really unlucky, he may come across the following problem:

Unit 2

Q **2.28** A player swears at the referee just before the kick-off. The referee decides to send him off for offensive language. Can he be substituted or must his team play with only ten players?

PART 4 • Law 4 – The players' equipment

The compulsory equipment of a player consists of: jersey or shirt; shorts; stockings; shinguards; footwear.

The main concern for the referee here is the safety of other players. It is important to make sure that players wear nothing that could be dangerous to themselves or other players. Items of jewellery such as earrings, pendants, rings and bracelets may well be considered as dangerous, and the referee should make certain that these have been removed or made safe before the start of play.

Question

(Answer on page 41.)

Q **2.29** A player is wearing a large ring that the referee considers dangerous. What action should be taken?

Frequently, a player's boots may be in a dangerous state, with sharp, burred edges on the studs. If this is the case, an otherwise harmless tackle may result in an injury.

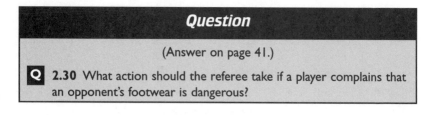

Question

(Answer on page 41.)

Q **2.30** What action should the referee take if a player complains that an opponent's footwear is dangerous?

Unit 2

It is important to remember that the players rely on the referee to do his best to ensure that the game is played safely. If he has any doubt, he has the right to inspect a player's footwear at any time.

Finally, in recent seasons the use of 'thermopants' or cycling shorts has grown. Players are allowed to use them, but they must be the same colour as the shorts the team is wearing. They must not extend further than the top of the knee. If a team is wearing multi-coloured shorts, the referee should judge whether the colour of the cycling shorts matches the *predominant* colour of the soccer shorts.

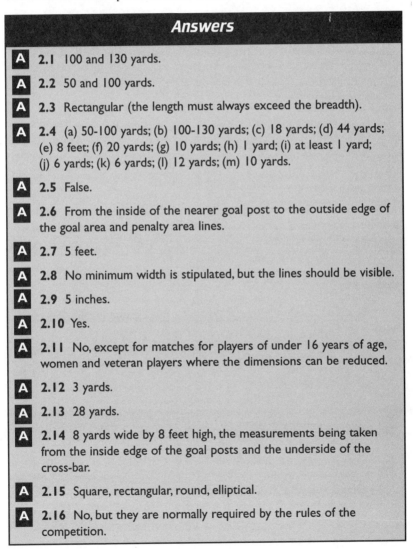

Answers

A **2.1** 100 and 130 yards.

A **2.2** 50 and 100 yards.

A **2.3** Rectangular (the length must always exceed the breadth).

A **2.4** (a) 50-100 yards; (b) 100-130 yards; (c) 18 yards; (d) 44 yards; (e) 8 feet; (f) 20 yards; (g) 10 yards; (h) 1 yard; (i) at least 1 yard; (j) 6 yards; (k) 6 yards; (l) 12 yards; (m) 10 yards.

A **2.5** False.

A **2.6** From the inside of the nearer goal post to the outside edge of the goal area and penalty area lines.

A **2.7** 5 feet.

A **2.8** No minimum width is stipulated, but the lines should be visible.

A **2.9** 5 inches.

A **2.10** Yes.

A **2.11** No, except for matches for players of under 16 years of age, women and veteran players where the dimensions can be reduced.

A **2.12** 3 yards.

A **2.13** 28 yards.

A **2.14** 8 yards wide by 8 feet high, the measurements being taken from the inside edge of the goal posts and the underside of the cross-bar.

A **2.15** Square, rectangular, round, elliptical.

A **2.16** No, but they are normally required by the rules of the competition.

Unit 2

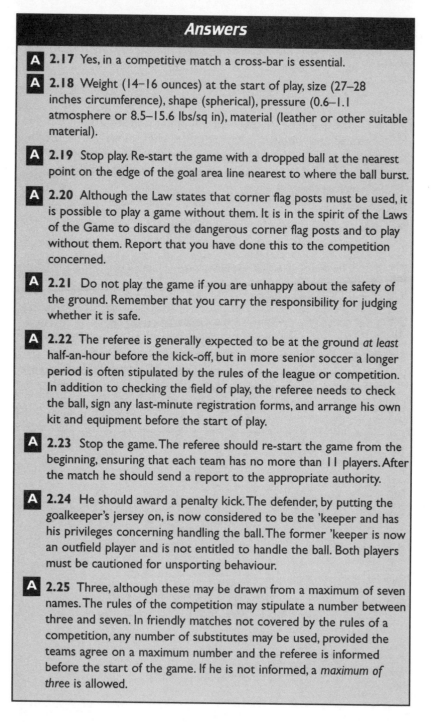

Answers

A **2.17** Yes, in a competitive match a cross-bar is essential.

A **2.18** Weight (14–16 ounces) at the start of play, size (27–28 inches circumference), shape (spherical), pressure (0.6–1.1 atmosphere or 8.5–15.6 lbs/sq in), material (leather or other suitable material).

A **2.19** Stop play. Re-start the game with a dropped ball at the nearest point on the edge of the goal area line nearest to where the ball burst.

A **2.20** Although the Law states that corner flag posts must be used, it is possible to play a game without them. It is in the spirit of the Laws of the Game to discard the dangerous corner flag posts and to play without them. Report that you have done this to the competition concerned.

A **2.21** Do not play the game if you are unhappy about the safety of the ground. Remember that you carry the responsibility for judging whether it is safe.

A **2.22** The referee is generally expected to be at the ground *at least* half-an-hour before the kick-off, but in more senior soccer a longer period is often stipulated by the rules of the league or competition. In addition to checking the field of play, the referee needs to check the ball, sign any last-minute registration forms, and arrange his own kit and equipment before the start of play.

A **2.23** Stop the game. The referee should re-start the game from the beginning, ensuring that each team has no more than 11 players. After the match he should send a report to the appropriate authority.

A **2.24** He should award a penalty kick. The defender, by putting the goalkeeper's jersey on, is now considered to be the 'keeper and has his privileges concerning handling the ball. The former 'keeper is now an outfield player and is not entitled to handle the ball. Both players must be cautioned for unsporting behaviour.

A **2.25** Three, although these may be drawn from a maximum of seven names. The rules of the competition may stipulate a number between three and seven. In friendly matches not covered by the rules of a competition, any number of substitutes may be used, provided the teams agree on a maximum number and the referee is informed before the start of the game. If he is not informed, a *maximum of three* is allowed.

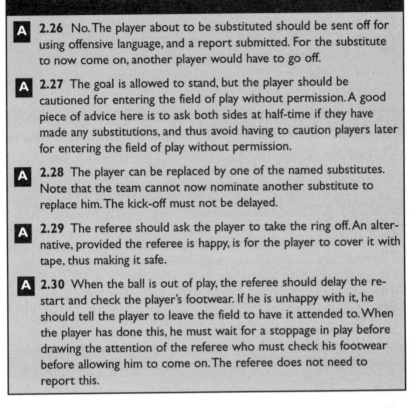

Answers

A **2.26** No. The player about to be substituted should be sent off for using offensive language, and a report submitted. For the substitute to now come on, another player would have to go off.

A **2.27** The goal is allowed to stand, but the player should be cautioned for entering the field of play without permission. A good piece of advice here is to ask both sides at half-time if they have made any substitutions, and thus avoid having to caution players later for entering the field of play without permission.

A **2.28** The player can be replaced by one of the named substitutes. Note that the team cannot now nominate another substitute to replace him. The kick-off must not be delayed.

A **2.29** The referee should ask the player to take the ring off. An alternative, provided the referee is happy, is for the player to cover it with tape, thus making it safe.

A **2.30** When the ball is out of play, the referee should delay the re-start and check the player's footwear. If he is unhappy with it, he should tell the player to leave the field to have it attended to. When the player has done this, he must wait for a stoppage in play before drawing the attention of the referee who must check his footwear before allowing him to come on. The referee does not need to report this.

UNIT 3

Laws 7–11

The Law states that a game should consist of two equal periods, normally of 45 minutes each. Under certain circumstances, such as fading light, the rules of the competition under which the game is being played may allow for it to be shorter than this, occasionally as little as 30 minutes each way. When this happens, there has to be a mutual agreement between the referee and the two clubs before the kick-off.

In some competitions, where the game must end in a result of victory to one of the teams, 'extra time' may have to be played. This consists of two equal halves, normally of a maximum of 15 minutes each.

Question

(Answer on page 56.)

Q 3.1 In an evening match, the referee plays 45 minutes in the first half but notices that the light is fading fast in the interval. Since the rules of the competition allow for games to last a total of 80 minutes, can he now play a second half of 35 minutes?

The Laws give players a right to a half-time break, but this should not be greater than 15 minutes. The duration of the half-time break should be stated in the rules of the competition that the game is being played under. Sometimes, when the weather is cold and miserable, and there is nowhere for players to shelter, everyone prefers to turn straight round at half-time and kick off for the second half. However, all players have a right to a half-time break, and they can take one if they so choose.

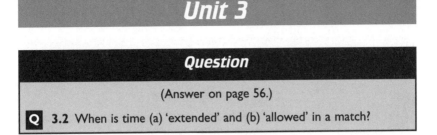

Unit 3

During a game, stoppages are likely to occur for substitutions, assessment of injury to players, removal of injured players from the field for treatment, and time wasting. Other causes might include the temporary loss of the ball, a sudden hailstorm or a floodlight failure. If this occurs, the referee is required to make an allowance in time to ensure that the game still lasts the full period.

It is possible that the referee will award a penalty kick just before the end of the first or second half. If this occurs, the referee must extend time to allow the kick to be taken or re-taken. This is dealt with more fully in Unit 5.

PART 2 • Law 8 – The start of play

The start of play is determined by bringing the team captains together for the toss of a coin. The winning captain has the choice of which end to defend. The other team is then allowed to take the kick-off. It is also necessary to toss for choice of ends after 90 minutes, if extra time is to be played.

Unit 3

Questions

(Answers on page 56.)

Q **3.4** What action should the referee take if the two captains refuse to shake hands just before the toss of the coin to decide kick-off?

Q **3.5** Where must all the players be located at the kick-off?

When the kick-off is taken, the players must be correctly positioned before the ball is in play. Therefore, the referee should place himself so that he is in a good position to view any encroachment that might occur. Opponents cannot come within 10 yards of the ball, or into the opponents' half, until it is kicked, *not* when the whistle is blown.

The ball must go *forwards* at the kick-off. If it does not, the kick is re-taken. The ball is in play once it has been kicked forwards. It must be touched by another player before it can be played again by the player taking the kick-off.

Question

(Answer on page 56.)

Q **3.6** At the kick-off the ball moves forwards, but is then kicked a second time by the same player before it has been touched by another player. What action should the referee take?

A kick-off is taken to start each half of the game, or each half of extra time when this is being played. It is used also to re-start the game after a goal has been scored.

At times the game has to be stopped by the referee when the ball is in play, as when a player is injured or if the ball deflates. When this occurs, the referee re-starts the game with a dropped ball from the place where the ball was when play was stopped. The referee should drop the ball from about waist height. As soon as it touches the ground, it is in play.

Unit 3

The dropped ball is a good reminder of the danger to the referee of keeping the whistle in his mouth when the game is in progress. There is always a chance that the ball will be kicked upwards towards the referee's face, and this may cause him to suffer a serious facial injury, with the whistle being driven through his teeth.

PART 3 • Law 9 – Ball in and out of play

The Law states that the ball is said to be 'out of play' in one of two circumstances.

1 When the ball has wholly crossed a goal line or touch line, whether on the ground or in the air.
2 When play has been stopped by the referee.

At all other times the ball is in play, including when it rebounds off the goal posts, cross-bar, corner flag posts, or the referee or his assistants when they are on the field of play.

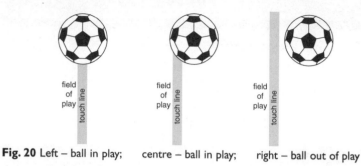

Fig. 20 Left – ball in play;   centre – ball in play;   right – ball out of play

For the ball to be out of play when it crosses over the goal or touch lines, the *whole* of the ball must go out of play. Since the lines are part of the field of play, so long as a *part* of the ball is in line with the markings, it is said to be still in play. Frequently this is not understood by players and managers even at the highest level. This can be seen in fig. 20.

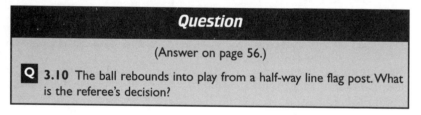

Question

(Answer on page 56.)

Q 3.10 The ball rebounds into play from a half-way line flag post. What is the referee's decision?

Unit 3

PART 4 • Law 10 – Method of scoring

The Law states that, for a goal to be awarded, the *whole* of the ball must cross the goal line, either on the ground or in the air, between the goal posts and under the cross-bar.

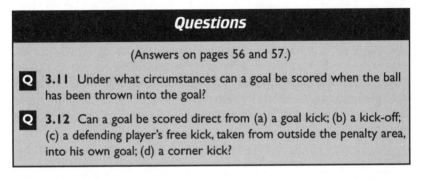

Questions

(Answers on pages 56 and 57.)

Q **3.11** Under what circumstances can a goal be scored when the ball has been thrown into the goal?

Q **3.12** Can a goal be scored direct from (a) a goal kick; (b) a kick-off; (c) a defending player's free kick, taken from outside the penalty area, into his own goal; (d) a corner kick?

It is important for the referee to bear in mind that it is impossible to award a goal if the ball has not *wholly* crossed the goal line. If, for example, a spectator or a dog or a ball from another game, comes on to the field, makes contact with the ball and prevents a certain goal, then the referee must stop the game and re-start with a dropped ball at the point where the ball made contact with the outside agent. Remember that this will be at the nearest point on the edge of the 6-yard area if the incident occurred in that area.

PART 5 • Law 11 – Offside

Although the offside Law is very brief, it has proved one of the most difficult and controversial for referees to enforce. There are several reasons for this.

Firstly, in recent years the game has become steadily faster, and this makes judging offside much more difficult. The assistant referees must be continually moving along the touch line to maintain a position in line with the last-but-one defender or the most advanced attacker, and this requires considerable concentration.

Secondly, the offside Law has become an important element of the tactics of a team, with defenders deliberately forcing attackers towards the middle of the field by moving up together. This has meant that offside decisions are critical to the result of the game, and form the basis of endless post-match debate. Even at the highest level, assistant referees have been shown to make crucial errors in judgement when the game is moving rapidly.

Thirdly, the Law contains the following words that place considerable pressure on the referee. *The player shall only be penalised if, at the moment the ball touches, or is played by one of his team, he is, in the opinion of the referee, involved in active play by: (a) interfering with play, or (b) interfering with an opponent, or (c) gaining an advantage by being in that position.* In other words, just being in an offside position is not sufficient to be judged offside. The referee has to make up his mind that the player is interfering with play or with an opponent, or seeking to gain an advantage, before he awards a free kick for offside.

For a player to be offside, initially he must be: (1) in his opponents' half, and (2) in front of the ball, i.e. he must be between the ball and the opponents' goal line. A player cannot therefore be judged offside if he is in his own half, or if he is behind the ball when it is played.

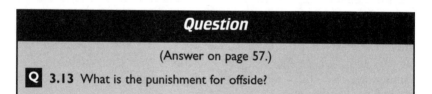

Question

(Answer on page 57.)

Q 3.13 What is the punishment for offside?

Assuming that the player fulfils the two conditions above, he can be judged offside if *at the moment the ball is played* by a member of his own side he has less than two defenders between himself and the opponents' goal line. Remember that he is not offside if he is in line with the last two defenders, or is in line with the last-but-one defender.

In fig. 21 the attacking player (A) has kicked the ball forwards to a colleague (B). Clearly, player B is in an offside position when the ball is played, and he is seeking to gain an advantage and interfering with play. The referee should thus penalise player B for being offside.

If player B has at least two defenders between him and the goal line at some point *after* the ball has been kicked, this makes no difference to the decision.

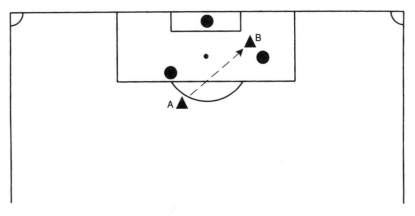

Fig. 21 Player B is offside

Player A in fig. 22 passes the ball forwards to player B. Player B runs forwards when the ball is kicked, and receives it in a position a few yards behind the two defenders. He is not offside because there were two defenders between him and the goal line when the ball was played.

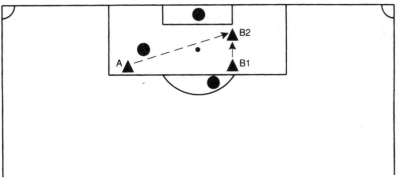

Fig. 22 Player B is not offside when the ball is played

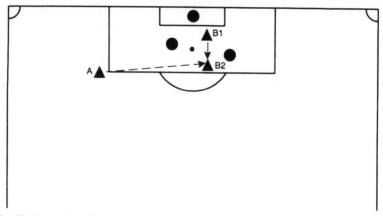

Fig. 23 Player B is offside when the ball is played

In fig. 23 the attacker, player B, runs back to receive the ball. Note that the player was offside when the ball was played, and since this is when offside is judged, the referee should penalise the attacker.

Note that a player cannot be judged offside if he is *level with* the last-but-one defender or with the last two defenders.

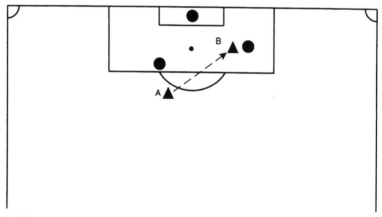

Fig. 24 Player B is not offside

In fig. 24 player A passes the ball to player B, who is in line with the last-but-one defender. Because he is in line with the player, he is not offside.

In each of these cases, where the player has been judged offside he is clearly interfering with play or seeking to gain an advantage. In practice, making this judgement is more complicated because on many occasions the player may be remote from the action and thus not interfering with play. A few examples can illustrate this problem.

Study fig. 25. Here, attacking player A passes the ball forwards to player B, who is clearly in an onside position. The colleague in the outside right position, player C, is clearly offside. Should the referee penalise the attacking team for offside? Most referees in this position would claim that player C was not interfering, or seeking to gain an advantage, but this depends on several factors. Has he taken a defender with him out to the wing? Is he near to the goal line and thus distracting the goalkeeper? Clearly, if the answer to these questions is yes, then the referee is more likely to penalise the forward. The problem is, where does the referee draw the line? If the player is only just inside his opponents' half, the situation is different from one in which he is close to the opponents' goal line. If he is very close to the touch line, this may be viewed differently from being closer to the centre of the field.

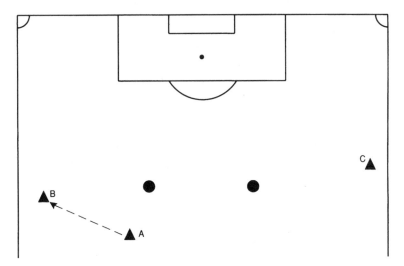

Fig. 25 When player A passes to B, should the referee penalise player C for being in an offside position, i.e. is he interfering with play or seeking to gain an advantage?

Unit 3

Q **3.14** Can a player be adjudged offside from: (a) a goal kick; (b) a corner kick; (c) a throw-in; (d) an indirect free kick taken by a colleague from his own penalty area; (e) a direct free kick awarded to his own side; (f) an opposing player's back pass?

Q **3.15** The referee waves play on because he does not consider an offside player to be interfering with play or seeking to gain an advantage. The player who receives the ball kicks for goal and the ball rebounds to the player who was offside, who now shoots for goal. What should the referee do?

Another, similar situation occurs when a player shoots for goal from a long distance, with a colleague standing in an offside position.

In fig. 26, player A shoots at goal from a position 35 yards from goal. His colleague (B) is a yard offside. Should the referee penalise him for being offside? In this situation most referees would claim that the player should not be penalised for being offside, unless he had distracted the defender nearby or the goalkeeper. In the next situation, however, the circumstances are rather more difficult.

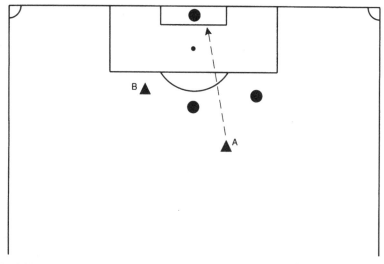

Fig. 26 When player A shoots at goal, should player B be ruled offside?

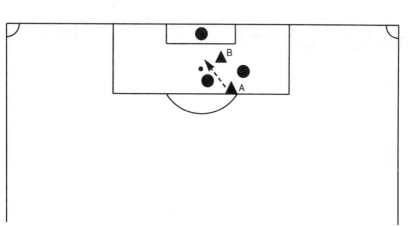

Fig. 27 Offside attacking player (B) moving nearer and nearer to the goal

Study fig. 27. As the offside attacking player (B) moves nearer and nearer to the goal, so it is more likely that he will be considered to be interfering with play. Here I am sure that most referees would give offside against him.

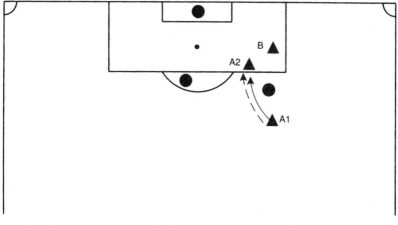

Fig. 28 When player A chips the ball around the defender and runs on to it, should player B be ruled offside?

Fig. 28 shows that the attacking player (A) has chipped the ball past the defender on his way to goal. His attacking colleague (B) is in an offside position. Offside can only be given when the ball is released. Therefore, if the attacking player retains control of the ball when dribbling it past a defender, it would be wrong to give offside because the ball has *not* been released. This can be difficult to judge if the attacker kicks the ball in the air about 20 yards forwards and chases on to it. Although the ball is not played by the colleague who is in an offside position, but by the original player, the referee must decide whether he retained possession when moving forwards. After all, the ball has been released by the attacker, even though he intends to and succeeds in regaining control of it. Once again, the referee must make his mind up, quickly and under pressure.

In the next situation (fig. 29), two players have broken through the defence. Player A shoots for goal. Should the referee penalise player B for being offside? Since player B is not seeking to interfere with play or an opponent, he should not be penalised and the goal should be allowed to stand.

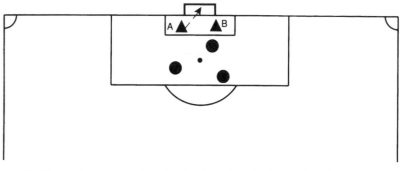

Fig. 29 Should player B be ruled offside when player A shoots at goal?

Recently, the International FA Board has tried to encourage attacking play by tilting the balance more in favour of attackers when offside is being judged. There is no doubt that soccer as a spectacle can be spoiled by teams playing with a defensive formation which is designed to constantly frustrate the opposition by making them offside continuously. This was not the original intention of the Law, and referees are now urged to only penalise when the player concerned is clearly involved in active play.

Using the assistant referees

Briefing the assistant referees has already been discussed in general terms in Unit 1. Of course, the assistant's job is particularly important in judging offside. Only by being exactly square to the most advanced attacker or last-but-one defender can the assistant properly judge offside. In refereeing local matches, the referee has to depend on club assistants, and here, as stated earlier, the quality of support he receives can vary considerably. A good assistant can make a game flow well, with players having confidence in his signals, and the referee able to delegate offside to him and thus concentrate on other aspects of the game. Quite often, however, the assistant has little interest in the job at all. Sometimes he may be the substitute, more interested in getting on the field than watching from the side lines. Sometimes he is the team secretary, trainer, treasurer and everything else rolled into one, and therefore does not always have his mind on the job in hand. It is worth remembering that being a club assistant referee can be a thankless job, and therefore even minimal support is appreciated by the referee.

When briefing the club assistant referee, it is good practice and important to the running of the game to try to make him feel involved. When he gives an offside signal he should be advised to stay with his flag raised until his signal has been acknowledged. If it is possible to play advantage, then the referee should do so, but he should always try to indicate to the assistant that his flag has been seen, and that the advantage is being applied.

On occasion it takes a few seconds for me to look over to see his signal. I remember once looking over to see if the assistant referee was giving offside and because I had taken my eyes off the game for two seconds, I missed a blatant handball in the penalty area. I learned from this lesson: now I warn the assistant referee that although he may be waving his flag for a while, he should stand his ground until I have clearly signalled to him. Failing to acknowledge him can lead to his becoming demoralised and he may lose interest, so don't forget!

From time to time, a team will provide a weak assistant referee and insist on playing the offside trap. This is very hard for the referee. My advice here is to talk to the team captain, and gently suggest that in the circumstances playing an offside trap may not be a very good idea, because errors are almost bound to occur.

Among all the Laws, offside is without doubt one of the most difficult for a referee to apply consistently. The higher speed of the game, the deliberate use of 'offside trap' tactics, poor support from club assistant referees, and an emphasis on the 'referee's opinion' in judging offside, make it a tough Law to apply well. Experience and fitness can go a long way in helping a referee to become proficient at applying offside.

Answers

A **3.1** The Law states clearly that the game should be of two *equal* periods. The referee cannot, therefore, play a 45-minute half followed by a 35-minute half. If in any doubt, the referee should err on the side of caution and play less time in the first half – having gained the agreement of the two captains, and subject to the rules of the competition.

A **3.2** Time should be *extended*, according to the Laws, only so that the taking of a penalty kick can be completed. Time should be *allowed* where it has been lost earlier in the game due to injury, substitutions, bad weather or other causes.

A **3.3** The referee does not have the power to decide the result of the game. The competition concerned will make a decision.

A **3.4** No action can be taken here. The captains are under no obligation to shake hands before the start of play.

A **3.5** At the kick-off, the players should be in their own half of the field of play, and in the case of the side not taking the kick-off, should be at least 10 yards from the ball. They must remain in these positions until the ball is in play.

A **3.6** Once the ball has rolled forwards, it is in play. If the kicker now plays the ball a second time, the referee must award an indirect free kick to the opposing team.

A **3.7** The ball cannot be played until it has touched the ground. The referee should stop play and re-start by dropping the ball again.

A **3.8** The Law does not make reference to the number of players who can be involved with a dropped ball. The convention is that one of each side challenges for the ball, but this is not stipulated.

A **3.9** No action should be taken. The assistant referee is part of the game, and play continues if the ball rebounds from him within the field of play.

A **3.10** Since the flag at the half-way line must be at least a yard from the touch line, the ball has gone out of play and the referee should award a throw-in.

A **3.11** Only when thrown by the attacking team's goalkeeper from his own penalty area, or thrown in to the goal by the defending team's goalkeeper.

Answers

A **3.12** (a) Yes, but only in the opponents' goal; (b) yes; (c) no – a goal cannot be scored direct into a player's own goal either from a direct or indirect free kick. The correct decision is a corner kick; (d) yes.

A **3.13** The punishment for offside is an indirect free kick to the defending side from the place where the opponent was standing when he was judged offside. If the offside was judged to have occurred in the goal area, the free kick can be taken from anywhere within that goal area. This applies to all free kicks to the defending side from inside that side's goal area.

A **3.14** (a) No; (b) no; (c) no; (d) yes; (e) yes; (f) no. Note that players cannot be offside if they receive the ball directly from a goal kick. Many teams are unaware of this, so that opponents place themselves in an offside position at a goal kick to take advantage of their ignorance.

A **3.15** Now that the player *has* gained an advantage, he can be penalised for offside. This is a problem area for the referee, who can find himself having to give an offside decision a while after the original offside. The player should only be penalised, however, if the offside occurs as part of the same movement in the game, and not if the original attack has broken down and a new one reformed.

UNIT 4

Fouls and misconduct

A well-known coach once said that the Laws of soccer were quite simple: 'If it moves kick it. If it doesn't move, kick it 'til it does.' In the minds of some players, perhaps this is not so far from the truth. Like any other sport, soccer reflects the society it is played in. The greater problems of man-management and match control created by a more aggressive society, with less respect for authority, are ones which the referee must come to terms with. This unit will consider the various offences which players might commit, and the way in which the referee should deal with them.

PART 1 • The penal offences

The Laws indicate that penal offences – described below – should be penalised by a direct free kick if committed against an opponent while the ball is in play. Note that deliberate handball is the only offence which is not committed *against* an opponent. The free kick should take place at the position where the incident occurred. If such an offence occurs within the penalty area and the offence is committed by a defender against an attacker, then a penalty kick should be awarded.

There are ten penal offences which are divided into two groups. The first six are offences which should only be punished when the player has committed the offence in a manner which the referee considers careless, reckless or involving excessive force. Note that this may happen even when the player has not necessarily intended to commit an offence. Until recently, it was essential for the referee to judge that the player had intentionally fouled an opponent. A recent change in the Laws has amended this, and now the referee must penalise the challenge if careless, even though there was no intent to foul the opponent.

Unit 4

Question

(Answer on page 83.)

Q **4.1** A player deliberately kicks an opponent with excessive force inside his own penalty area while the ball is in play in the other half of the field of play. What should the referee do?

(1) Kicking or attempting to kick an opponent

If a player makes no attempt to play the ball, but deliberately kicks an opponent, the referee should award a direct free kick or, where appropriate, a penalty kick to the opposition. Note that the kick does not have to make contact for this to happen. An *attempted* kick is sufficient for the referee to take action.

If the opponent is kicked in the process of a player making a fair tackle in which the ball is played cleanly, the player should not be penalised, unless the referee felt that excessive force or recklessness was involved.

Fig. 30 Kicking an opponent

Occasionally, a player lifts his studs and goes 'over the ball' in a tackle. This is a particularly dangerous tackle in which the opponent can suffer a serious injury if the tackler makes contact. If the referee sees this occur, then he must take action, usually by sending off the player (according to the severity of the offence).

(2) Tripping or attempting to trip an opponent

A tripping offence is often committed by a player when all hope of making contact with the ball has gone, and his only hope is to bring down the opponent unfairly. Tripping refers not just to the use of the leg or foot, but also to the use of the body by stooping either behind or in front of the opponent. As with kicking an opponent, simply *attempting* to trip an opponent is a penal offence.

Fig. 31 Tripping, by stooping in front of or behind an opponent

Fig. 32 Tripping, using the legs

(3) Jumping at an opponent

A player may jump at an opponent in a number of ways. He may, for example, jump with both feet at the opponent. It is also possible for the player to jump at the opponent using his whole body, knocking him over or forcing him off the ball in the process.

(4) Charging an opponent

It is possible to quite legally charge an opponent but only when the ball is in playing distance, when both players are trying to play the ball, and when the charge is made with the shoulder to the opponent's shoulder. If the charge is violent, involving excessive force, then the player must be penalised by a direct free kick (or penalty kick). A dangerous charge occurs when it is directed against a different part of the opponent's body, such as the middle of the back. Such a charge, even if applied with minimal force, is likely to knock the opponent off-balance at best, and, at worst, cause some physical injury.

Fig. 33 Fair charge

Fig. 34 Charge in the back

Fig. 35 Charging in a violent or dangerous manner

As we have seen already, a player may not charge an opponent in the small of the back. It is possible to charge an opponent from behind if the opponent is impeding him, but only if the charge is broadly aimed at the shoulder area of the opponent. If the opponent is *not* impeding the player, he may not be charged in this way. Note that when the opponent is shielding the ball, which is under his control, he is *not* penalised.

(5) Striking or attempting to strike an opponent

As with kicking or attempting to kick an opponent, the player does not have to actually make contact in order for a free kick to be awarded for this offence. A wild swing is sufficient for the referee to award a direct free kick or, when appropriate, a penalty kick. Frequently, the referee will send a player off for striking an opponent, because this is normally construed as serious foul play.

Fig. 36 Striking or attempting to strike an opponent.

Question

(Answer on page 83.).

Q **4.2** A corner kick is taken. With the ball in the air above the penalty area, a defender and an attacker roll over the goal line into the goal where the defender punches the attacker and the attacker retaliates by head-butting him. What action should the referee take, and how should he re-start the game?

(6) Pushing an opponent
Frequently, a player will push an opponent in order to stop him from playing, or competing for, the ball. A player might attempt to hide such a push from behind, and it may be hard for the referee to spot, particularly if the players are close together and the ball is being kicked into play from a goal kick, for example. The referee is advised to stand square to the players in this situation so that he can judge whether this offence is occurring.

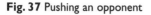

Fig. 37 Pushing an opponent   **Fig. 38** Pulling an opponent's shirt – a holding offence

The following four penal offences should be punished with a direct free kick, or penalty kick if appropriate, but the question of whether the player was careless, reckless or used excessive force is not a consideration.

(7) Making contact with an opponent before touching the ball
The Law requires that a player should be penalised if he makes contact with an opponent, before contact has been made with the ball. An example of this is the sliding tackle. This is allowed if it is not dangerous, but if the player fails to make contact with the ball, and trips his opponent, then this is penalised by a direct free kick. The player must also be cautioned when this occurs. If the tackle is violent, and from behind, with little or no attempt to play the ball, then the offending player should be sent off.

(8) Spitting at an opponent
It is hardly necessary to have to point out the need for referees to deal severely with this offence. Not only is a direct free kick awarded, but the offending player must also be sent off.

(9) Holding an opponent
In desperation, a player might hold an opponent by grabbing his shirt or arm, but holding can occur in other ways. For example, with both players on the floor following a tackle, a player might grip the

opponent's ankle or his legs to prevent him from getting up and playing the ball. Another example is where a forward puts his arm out, apparently to steady himself, but holds his opponent off to gain an unfair advantage by stopping him from tackling fairly for the ball. If two opponents have fallen over following a challenge, and one deliberately uses his legs to stop the other from getting up, he should also be penalised for holding.

(10) Handling the ball

Outfield players must be penalised for deliberately handling the ball. They may handle the ball unintentionally and not be penalised. Deliberate handball is often described as 'hand to ball', but 'ball to hand' is where this happens accidentally. Of course, it is often very difficult to judge this precisely; a grey area occurs where the referee has to make up his mind as to whether the player has *deliberately* handled the ball.

Question

(Answer on page 83.)

Q **4.3** A player is sitting in his own penalty area putting his boot back on. The ball is kicked towards goal by an opponent, whereupon the player lifts his boot and uses it to re-direct the ball over the crossbar. What action should the referee take?

Remember that the goalkeeper is allowed to handle the ball within his own penalty area so long as he does not retain it for more than six seconds.

Questions

(Answers on page 83.)

Q **4.4** The goalkeeper, standing outside his own penalty area, reaches out and handles the ball inside his own penalty area. What action should the referee take?

Q **4.5** The goalkeeper, standing inside the penalty area, reaches outside the area and handles the ball. What action should the referee now take?

Questions cont.

Q **4.6** A player did not deliberately handle the ball but gains an advantage as the ball bounces kindly for him. What action should the referee take?

When deliberate handball offences occur, they must be punished by the award of a direct free kick or a penalty kick as appropriate. In addition to this, the referee might consider cautioning or sending off the offending player, depending on the circumstances in which this occurs. This is dealt with in Part 4 of this unit.

Question

(Answer on page 83.)

Q **4.7** A player commits a penal offence by tripping an opponent in the penalty area. The penalty kick is scored. Does this cancel out the need for the referee to take the offending player's name and report him for misconduct?

It is important to commit to memory the ten penal offences.

The Ten Penal Offences

When committed in a manner considered by the referee to be careless, reckless, or involving excessive force	(1) Kicking or attempting to kick an opponent.
	(2) Tripping or attempting to trip an opponent.
	(3) Jumping at an opponent.
	(4) Charging an opponent.
	(5) Striking or attempting to strike an opponent.
	(6) Pushing an opponent.
Whenever committed	(7) Making contact with an opponent before touching the ball, when tackling.
	(8) Spitting at an opponent.
	(9) Holding an opponent.
	(10) Deliberately handling the ball.

PART 2 • Non-penal offences

There are several offences for which the correct award is an indirect free kick, i.e. a kick from which a goal *cannot* be scored direct, but which must be played by another player first.

(1) Playing in a dangerous manner
This is defined as play which, while in itself not against the spirit of the game, is dangerous to an opponent. A good example of this is when a player attempts to kick a ball at shoulder height. If no opponent is near him, this action would not be dangerous. However, if an opponent was attempting to play the ball with his head, behaviour which would be reasonable if it was at that height, the action by the player would be dangerous. This is illustrated in fig. 39.

Fig. 39 Dangerous play

If this occurs, the referee should award an indirect free kick to the non-offending side.

A similar incident may occur when the ball is around waist height. What action should the referee take here? Since it is reasonable to attempt to kick the ball at this height, and similarly reasonable to attempt to head it, it is problematical whether a free kick for dangerous play should be awarded in this situation.

Unit 4

Consider the following situation.

Question

(Answer on page 83.)

Q **4.8** A player who has fallen over following a tackle raises himself off the ground and tries to head the ball just a couple of feet off the ground as an opponent tries to kick the ball. What action should the referee take in this case?

Other forms of dangerous play can occur. For example, the goalkeeper may be coming out to collect the ball and is challenged by an attacker. While the attacker can reasonably attempt to play the ball, if he launches himself at it when the goalkeeper is near he may place the latter in considerable danger. Once again, an indirect free kick should be awarded if the referee judges that the attacker has played in a dangerous manner.

It is important to remember that the referee must decide whether this is the lesser offence of dangerous play or the more serious one of charging.

(2) Impeding the progress of an opponent

Impeding, formerly known as intentional obstruction, is defined in the Laws as: . . . *when not playing the ball, impeding the progress of an opponent, i.e. running between the opponent and ball, or interposing the body so as to form an obstacle to an opponent.* It is perfectly reasonable, however, for a player to put his body between the opponent and the ball so long as the ball remains within playing distance.

If the ball is *not* within playing distance, the player is guilty of impeding. Often, a player who has failed to win a tackle might impede an opponent in desperation. On occasion, if a ball is passed through towards the goalkeeper, a defender might impede an opponent to stop him from challenging fairly for the ball.

Impeding might deny the opponent a clear opportunity to score a goal. When this occurs, despite the fact that only an indirect free kick is awarded, the referee will have to send off the offending player. This scenario is dealt with later in this unit. It is important to bear in mind that impeding does not have to be deliberate. Simply by being in the way of an opponent is sufficient for the referee to penalise this offence.

Fig. 40 Impeding

(3) Preventing the goalkeeper from releasing the ball from his hands

An opponent may not impede the goalkeeper nor prevent him from releasing the ball. An indirect free kick should be awarded against the offender.

(4) The goalkeeper not releasing the ball into play properly

Over the past few years the Law has been changed several times in an attempt to ensure that goalkeepers do not waste time but release the ball into play as quickly as possible.

(i) Once the goalkeeper takes control of the ball with his hands, he must release the ball into play within six seconds

A change in the Laws for season 2000/1 abolished the 'Four Steps Law' whereby the goalkeeper could take a maximum of four steps while holding the ball. The Law now requires the goalkeeper on gaining possession of the ball to release it into play within six seconds. He can take as many steps as he likes within the six-second period.

In an effort to reduce defensive play, it is against the Law for a goalkeeper to pick up the ball when it has been deliberately passed with the feet by a colleague. It is also an offence for the goalkeeper to receive the ball into his hands from a team-mate's throw-in.

Questions

(Answers on pages 83.)

Q **4.9** A player heads the ball into the arms of his goalkeeper. What action should the referee take?

Q **4.10** The ball is deliberately kicked back to the goalkeeper by one of his colleagues. What action should the referee take if the goalkeeper: (a) picks the ball up; (b) plays the ball with his feet?

Note that passing the ball is not, in itself, an offence, but picking it up is, and should be penalised by the award of an indirect free kick from where the offence occurred. It is normally perfectly acceptable for a player to head or chest the ball to his goalkeeper. If, however, this is done to get round the Law, for example with one defender chipping the ball up in the air, and another heading it on to the goalkeeper, then this is an offence. The defender who headed the ball back should be penalised, and an indirect free kick awarded against him from the place where the offence occurred. The defender is also cautioned for unsporting behaviour.

(ii) The goalkeeper is not permitted to touch the ball again with his hands after he has released it from his possession if the ball has not touched any other player
If the goalkeeper controls the ball with his hands, and then plays it with his feet, but then again picks it up or otherwise controls it with his hands, the referee should award an indirect free kick.

(iii) The goalkeeper is not permitted to touch the ball with his hands after it has been deliberately kicked to him by a colleague
If the ball is clearly passed to the goalkeeper by a colleague, he may play the ball with his feet, but if he picks the ball up an indirect free kick must be awarded against him.

(iv) The goalkeeper is not permitted to touch the ball with his hands after he has received it directly from a throw-in taken by a colleague
This is self-explanatory. Once again, the referee must award an indirect free kick against the goalkeeper.

(v) The goalkeeper is not permitted to waste time
Once the goalkeeper has control of the ball in his hands, he must release the ball into play. An indirect free kick is awarded if he holds the ball for more than six seconds. Note that in each case, the indirect free kick should be taken from the place where the offence occurred.

(vi) Commits any other offence, not previously mentioned in Law 12, for which play is stopped to caution or dismiss a player
This is straightforward. For example, if the referee stops the game to caution a player for unsporting behaviour, or sends a player off for foul language, the game is re-started with an indirect free kick to be taken from where the offence occurred.

Unit 4

(Answer on page 83.)

Q **4.11** The goalkeeper receives a pass, with his feet, from a colleague and dribbles the ball across the edge of the penalty area. An opponent complains to the referee that the goalkeeper is wasting time and should be penalised by the award of an indirect free kick. What action, if any, should the referee take?

The 'professional foul' – unfairly denying a goalscoring opportunity

In an attempt to penalise cynical, unfair play and to crack down on cheating, the Laws have become much tougher on this type of offence in recent years. A player who is facing an open goal and a good goalscoring opportunity, receives a lesser award if he is given a free kick or a penalty following a so-called 'professional foul' which robs him of his chance on goal. Similarly, if a player deliberately handles the ball to deny a good goalscoring opportunity, the referee is required to take firm action against the player. This can be summarised as follows.

• An attacking player is fouled by an opponent and in the referee's opinion is denied a goalscoring opportunity.
Action
The player shall be sent off the field of play for serious foul play.

• A defender deliberately handles the ball, in an attempt to stop an obvious goalscoring opportunity.
Action
(i) If a goal is *not* scored, send the player off for serious foul play.

(ii) If a goal *is* scored, despite the defender's action, caution the player concerned for unsporting behaviour.

It is important to remember that the judgement of the referee is crucial here. It is up to him to decide that a clear goalscoring opportunity has been denied. If it has, then he *must* send the offending player off. If it has not, then he may send off or caution the offending player, according to his judgement of the severity of the foul.

Unit 4

So far we have considered offences committed by players on opponents, or by the goalkeeper when in possession of the ball. There are other offences which may occur in a game where the offending player has not committed an offence against an opponent, but where the referee has to penalise. In these cases, the correct way to re-start the game is normally with an indirect free kick.

(1) An assault by a player on a colleague, official or spectator
Occasionally, players from the same side will come into conflict. If this happens, the referee may have to stop the game to send off or caution the players concerned. When he has done this, he should re-start the game with an indirect free kick to the non-offending side, to be taken from where the incident occurred. If this is within the goal area, it must be taken from the nearest point on the line parallel to the goal line if two defending players were involved, or from anywhere within the area if the offending players were attackers.

From time to time a spectator may come on to the pitch, resulting in an assault by a player. In this case the referee should again deal with the player(s) concerned and re-start with an indirect free kick. If an assistant referee or the referee is assaulted, then once again an indirect free kick is the correct way to re-start the game. Remember, however, that if the referee is assaulted, it may be unwise to re-start the game if he has suffered injury or shock. This problem is dealt with later in this unit.

Question

(Answer on page 83.)

Q 4.12 A player leaves the field of play, and while the game is continuing, assaults a spectator. What action should the referee take and how should the game be re-started?

(2) An act of unsporting behaviour
Sometimes a player will commit an offence which will give his team an unfair advantage, and where the referee needs to penalise his team for this. There are several situations where this might occur.

(i) Distracting the opposition by calling for the ball

Occasionally a player will shout 'My ball!' or 'Leave it!' when attempting to gain control of the ball. Opponents may be confused by this and decide not to challenge for the ball. It is rarely a deliberate ploy by the player, but it may give an unfair advantage. This is classed as unsporting behaviour and, if play has been stopped, it should be re-started by the award of an indirect free kick. The player must also be cautioned.

Sometimes a player will simply shout or yell in an attempt to distract an opponent. This represents unsporting behaviour and is punished by the award of an indirect free kick to the other side if play has not been stopped, and the player concerned cautioned.

Question

(Answer on page 84.)

Q 4.13 A player is standing 5 yards behind a colleague when the ball comes in his direction. Seeing his colleague move to intercept the ball, he shouts 'Leave it!' There are no opponents close to play. What action should the referee take?

This problem is more frequently found among less experienced players. The referee should advise players to use a name, so that they shout 'John Smith's ball!' or 'Goalkeeper's ball!' to avoid confusion.

(ii) Climbing on the back of a colleague

Sometimes a player will climb on the back of a colleague to gain height when heading the ball. This is unsporting and gives an unfair advantage to his side. The referee will award an indirect free kick to the other side when this occurs, and caution the offending player.

(iii) Dissent

Sometimes a player will dissent from a refereeing decision with the ball still in play. This can be either by word or action. The referee will stop the game to issue the caution, and re-start with an indirect free kick to the opposition from where the offence occurred, subject to the proviso made earlier when the offence occurs in the goal area.

(iv) Deceit

Players who try to deceive the referee in an effort to gain a decision in favour of their team should be sanctioned for unsporting behaviour.

Unit 4

PART 4 • Dealing with misconduct

A referee once wrote: 'If you can keep your head while those around are losing theirs and blaming it on you, you've just missed the most blatant foul in the whole game.'

'Keeping your head' is the most important skill the referee needs when dealing with misconduct by players. Mistakes made here may inflame an already difficult and tense situation, and the referee needs good man-management skills if he is to maintain a calm control and the continued respect of the players.

The most important advice here is to aim at *prevention* rather than *cure*. An unfair tackle early in the game, or a bit of 'needle' developing between two players, can often be nipped in the bud quickly by a quiet, or, if necessary, a not so quiet word of warning and a free kick. Failure to pick up such problems can result in escalating problems later in the game. A recent survey of misconduct in my region showed that less experienced referees were more likely to caution or send off players than more experienced officials. There may be several reasons for this, but I am sure that inexperienced referees are less likely to spot the seeds of trouble in their early stages, and thus are forced to take more punitive action later.

Often, a quiet warning can have good effect. It shows the player that the referee is aware of what he has done and that he is not prepared to accept this behaviour. When speaking to a player, the referee should not lecture him in an arrogant or irritable way, but calmly let him know the position and warn him accordingly. I also believe that it is better to speak quietly and discreetly to him, rather than bawling him out in front of others. If the referee can do so in the course of the game, so much the better.

Above all, he should never touch a player. This can cause considerable offence. The referee has no right to do this and it may encourage the player to touch the referee back a little more aggressively. The referee should be firm and fair, treating the player with respect, but not leaving him in any doubt as to what he is expected to do.

Finally, the referee should never make a threat that he might not carry out. He should never say 'I'm sending off any player who swears in this game' unless he really *does* intend to do so. If the referee fails to be true to his word, he will lose the respect of the players very quickly.

Unit 4

Cautions and sendings off

At some time, it becomes necessary to take a player's name and report him for misconduct, either by issuing him with a caution or by sending him off. For less serious offences, a caution is given and the player's misdeeds are reported on a caution report form. A player can be cautioned and shown the yellow card if he commits any of the following offences:

- Is guilty of unsporting behaviour.
- Shows dissent by word or action.
- Persistently infringes the Laws of the Game.
- Delays the re-start of play.
- Fails to respect the required distance when play is re-started with a corner kick or free kick.
- Enters or re-enters the field of play without the referee's permission.
- Deliberately leaves the field of play without the referee's permission.

Unsporting behaviour

This is by far the most common reason for cautioning a player since the term covers every type of minor villainy. A deliberate and hard foul tackle, cheating in some form, holding a player, and many other offences, are punished by a caution under this heading. This does not mean that the referee must *always* caution a player who commits one of these offences. He must make a decision based on the severity of the offence. A hard two-footed tackle, for example, aimed at an opponent, should result normally in a caution, while a late tackle in which the opponent narrowly got to the ball before the offending player, might not. The referee might consider that a 'quiet word' of warning would suffice. Remember, however, that there is a limit to the number of 'quiet words' the referee can reasonably have with a player before deciding to caution him.

Dissent

Dissent from the referee's decision is often verbal, with the player simply complaining about a decision. Occasionally it takes the form of some action, such as petulantly kicking the ball away after a decision by the referee, or making a gesture such as waving the arms in disgust. When this happens, the referee should caution the player concerned.

Unit 4

Question

(Answer on page 84.)

Q **4.14** The referee awards a free kick. After the kick is taken and the ball is in play, a player complains to the referee about the decision. The referee decides to caution him for dissent but has to stop the game to do this. How is the game re-started?

A useful piece of advice here is for the referee to try to avoid trouble before it occurs. Once again, prevention is better than cure. Often you will notice how the referee in a professional game will run to the centre circle after a goal is scored *before* recording the goal in his notebook. This does not guarantee that players will not show dissent, but they will have to run to the centre circle to do so. Players often do foolish things in the heat of the moment, but calm down very quickly. Staying in the penalty area might invite a player to make a comment which might be avoided if the referee has gone some distance away.

Question

(Answer on page 84.)

Q **4.15** A player deliberately grabs an opponent's shirt, but the referee allows the advantage. Play continues for a further 3 minutes before the ball goes out of play. Can the referee now caution the offending player?

Persistently infringing the Laws
The use of this heading for a caution applies to a situation in which a player commits a string of small but irritating offences, each of which is individually too minor to merit a caution for unsporting behaviour. An example of this would be a player challenging an opponent carelessly and then later deliberately impeding. Each offence, in itself, is minor, but when taken together the player is unfairly distracting the opposition.

Delaying the re-start of play
A player may deliberately delay the start of play by, for example, refusing to release the ball to the opponents, or by standing over the ball and preventing the opponent from kicking it. If this occurs the player concerned must be cautioned.

Failing to respect the required distance when play is re-started with a corner kick or free kick

Occasionally an opponent will stand less than 10 yards from the ball when the opposition have been awarded a free kick or corner kick. This gives him an unfair advantage over his opponents and he will be cautioned. Bear in mind that some common sense is needed here. Players should be told where they should stand. They should be cautioned only when they deliberately attempt to gain an unfair advantage.

Entering or re-entering the field of play without permission

It is quite rare that a player will intentionally enter or re-enter the field without permission. If one does, however, he must be cautioned.

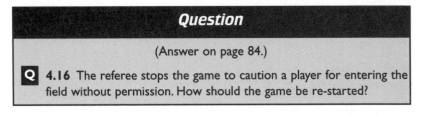

Question

(Answer on page 84.)

Q **4.16** The referee stops the game to caution a player for entering the field without permission. How should the game be re-started?

Occasionally a team will forget to tell the referee that a substitution has been made at half-time. When this occurs, the referee will caution the player who has entered the field without permission. As stated earlier, prevention is better than cure, so it is good practice to ask each side if they have introduced any substitutes before the second half commences.

Finally, it is a good idea to count the players before the start of the game. This is partly to make sure that each team does not have *more* than 11 players, and partly to see if they have *fewer* than 11. Of course, the team *can* start with fewer than 11 players, and if this is so the additional players can join at any time. If the referee is aware of this fact, he can simply wave on the late-arriving players at an appropriate point in the game. Failure to count the players before the start might lead to confusion in the referee's mind as he may wonder why further players wish to join the side later in the game.

Deliberately leaving the field of play without permission

A player is cautioned if he leaves the field of play without permission. Referees should use some common sense here. If a player is clearly injured and steps over the touch line to receive attention while the ball is in play at the other end of the field, it would be harsh to caution him for this offence since he may not have been able to attract the referee's attention. Bear in mind that he must still get the referee's permission to re-enter the field of play, however.

Sending off offences

Players can be sent off for offences under seven headings.

1 Serious foul play.
2 Violent conduct.
3 Spitting at an opponent or any other person.
4 Denying an opponent a goal or obvious goalscoring opportunity by deliberately handling the ball.
5 Denying an obvious goalscoring opportunity to an opponent moving towards the offender's goal by committing an offence punishable by a free kick or penalty kick.
6 Using offensive, insulting or abusive language or gestures.
7 Receiving a second caution in the same match.

When a player is sent off, the offender must be shown the red card and must then leave the field. He is forbidden to take any further part in the game.

Questions

(Answers on page 84.)

Q **4.17** If during a game a referee cautions a player and at the conclusion of the match the player sincerely apologises, should the referee decide not to submit the report?

Q **4.18** With the ball in play, a player punches a colleague who retaliates by head-butting him. The referee stops the game and sends both players off. How does the referee re-start the game?

Incidents involving violence are usually the most explosive, and may require swift and decisive action by the referee. The offending players should be dealt with quickly and efficiently. If two players have been involved in a fight, and they are both being sent off, the referee should try to ensure that they return to the dressing room by different routes, or perhaps with a delay between them to stop the fight from re-commencing as they leave the field of play.

Unit 4

(1) Serious foul play
A referee must distinguish between what he considers to be 'foul play' and 'serious foul play'. Broadly speaking, serious foul play occurs when a player commits a physical act of excessive force or violence, committed with the clear intention of hurting an opponent or stopping him from either completing a skilful move or scoring a goal. Offences here may thus include the 'over-the-top tackle' in which an opponent raises his foot over the ball in a tackle, and thus digs his studs into the other player's leg. Essentially, serious foul play is defined as misconduct of a serious nature against an opponent in a playing situation. In recent years, the meaning of the term 'serious foul play' has been broadened to include a foul tackle aimed at denying an opponent an obvious goalscoring opportunity. This includes a situation in which a player deliberately trips or pushes an opponent, but also when a player deliberately handles the ball to stop it entering the goal or reaching an opponent who is placed in a strong position to score.

(2) Violent conduct
Violent conduct refers to misconduct of an extreme nature against opponents when *not* in a playing situation or against a colleague, officials or spectators at any time.

(3) Spitting at an opponent or any other person
Clearly, spitting is a serious offence and should be treated as such by the referee. Any player guilty of this must be immediately sent off.

(4) Denying an opponent a goal or an obvious goalscoring opportunity by deliberately handling the ball
As was discussed in Part 2 of this unit, deliberate handball to deny an obvious goalscoring opportunity must be punished by the sending off of the offender. The referee must be reasonably certain that a goal would otherwise have been scored. Remember that if the offending player attempts to deny the opportunity but fails and a goal is scored, he is only cautioned.

(5) Denying an obvious goalscoring opportunity to an opponent moving towards the player's goal by an offence punishable by a free kick or a penalty kick
If a player commits such an offence he should be shown the red card and sent off the field of play. Note that it is essential for the referee to use his judgement here as to whether there was a clear goalscoring opportunity.

(6) Using offensive, insulting or abusive language or gestures

The Laws require the referee to send off players who use such offensive language or gestures. This does not necessarily have to be directed at the referee or be obscene. FIFA are keen to remove racism from soccer. Racist remarks should be dealt with severely and the offender sent off.

(7) Receiving a second caution in the same match

Once a player has received a caution, the committing of a second cautionable offence is punished by the player being sent off. This can occur when, for example, a player commits dissent and is then guilty of unsporting behaviour.

Cautioning or sending off a player

It is a good idea to use some tact and diplomacy here. The player is likely to be agitated or upset, so if the referee really wants to make him more volatile, he will find it very easy to do so. It is important to be clear and firm, and not to show anger or irritation.

If the referee wishes to take a player's name, and the player has moved some distance away, there is a temptation to blow the whistle and order the player over. This could well enrage him and, in any case, can be very embarrassing for the referee if he refuses to come. On the other hand, it is not a good idea to chase the player across the field and end up facing him completely out of breath. It is best to try to meet the player half-way. The referee should ask him to come over, and then walk towards him without rushing.

When the referee meets the player, he must ask for his full name and explain to him that he is being cautioned or sent off. It is not necessary to give every detail of why he is being cautioned, but just the heading. Experienced referees often tell a player that he is being cautioned *before* asking his name, to calm him down if he was expecting to be sent off. But a player should not be told he is being sent off until his name has been noted because this gives him less opportunity to argue with the referee or become aggressive.

It is important to get the player's *full* name. Sometimes a player will refuse to give his name, or even give an obviously false name. If a player refuses to co-operate, it is a good idea to ask him to take a deep breath and take his time. Often, players calm down after a few seconds. If they continue to refuse to give their name, it is possible to send the report in with no name. This is very unusual, and players and their clubs generally realise that the governing body will pursue them to discover the name of the offending player. They also face the problem that any fines imposed are likely to be higher.

If a player gives an absurd name, the referee should ask him to reconsider, but if he insists the name given should be written down. It is worth remembering that a handful of players do have names that appear unbelievable. For example, in my experience there really was once a player called Donald Duck!

Using red and yellow cards

To make clear his decision to spectators and to players and club officials, it is necessary that the referee shows a yellow card when cautioning a player and a red one when sending a player off. The card should be held high with the arm vertical, after the player's name has been taken. When a player is being sent off following a second cautionable offence, the referee should first show a yellow card, and then a red card, to make it clear that the player has committed a second cautionable offence, rather than a sending off offence.

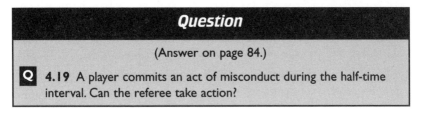

Question

(Answer on page 84.)

Q **4.19** A player commits an act of misconduct during the half-time interval. Can the referee take action?

Misconduct by club officials and spectators

From time to time, the referee has to deal with club officials who are abusive or threatening, or who otherwise misbehave. If the referee feels that action beyond a verbal warning is required, then he should take the name of the person concerned and report the misbehaviour accordingly. I have only had to send in a report on a manager on one occasion, when the gentleman concerned had not kept fully up to date with the changes in the Law on the goalkeeper's possession of the ball. After remonstrating with me and ignoring my warnings, he continued to argue and became abusive, so I had little alternative but to ask for his name. If it is possible to warn the official then do so. Sometimes, removing the official from the dug-out and into the stand may solve the problem.

A club is responsible for its spectators. If they are unruly or violent, then this too can be reported and the club will be asked to account for the incident. This is difficult when a game is being played on a local park to which anyone can have access. Where a club charges admission, however, the situation is very different. The club has a duty to take whatever action it can to ensure good behaviour by its supporters.

Unit 4

Filling in the report

Perhaps the most unpopular and arduous task faced by the referee is that of completing a misconduct report form. In fact, this is so arduous a task that a minority of referees fail to send them in at all! This is a serious omission, much frowned upon by the authorities, and for good reason. If referees fail to send in reports, this makes things more difficult for subsequent referees at that team's games. The assumption is that other referees will also have a double standard here, and will be prepared to overlook misconduct. It can also rebound very badly on a referee when reports are not handed in on players who have been cautioned or sent off and where this becomes known.

A colleague once sent a player off and failed to submit a report, an action which led to his career eventually collapsing. Normally, a copy of the report is sent by the County FA to the club concerned, for its information and any relevant comments. When the club had heard nothing, it wrote and asked if, perhaps, the report had been lost in the post, and if another copy could be sent as they wished to appeal. Of course, the FA had no record of the incident and thus wrote to the referee for his observations. The FA then suspended him and, ultimately, his once promising career was finished, and he was dropped from the senior league in which he was then refereeing.

While filling in misconduct reports can be time-consuming and awkward, it is essential that the referee spends some time and effort on this chore. At best, mistakes are embarrassing and humiliating; at worst, players may appeal successfully if errors are apparent in the report. Referees are encouraged to follow a simple procedure.

1 Quote the *full* name of the player and his club, and use first names. There may be more than one J. Smith in a team, so the use of a player's full name is necessary to avoid confusion.
2 The offence for which the player is being cautioned or sent off must be clearly stated. This is made easier by the layout of the form, and simply requires the referee to fill in a letter in the appropriate box.
3 Clearly but briefly state what happened. The report does not require a deep discussion of the game or other incidents, but simply a description of the offence for which the player is being reported. The referee should try to be both precise and concise.
4 The referee should state the *time* that the incident occurred, *where* it occurred, and his own position at the time.

5 Reports must be submitted in duplicate, with a third copy retained by the referee for reference. This is important if there is an appeal by the player that results in a personal hearing that the referee will be expected to attend to answer questions about his actions.

6 It is important to check spelling and grammar in the report. The best advice here is to write the report out in rough to start with, before entering it on to the report form. Mistakes here may make the referee look foolish when the report is received by the club.

7 Some associations insist that each separate incident needs a separate report. This means that if the referee has cautioned a player early in the game, and sent him off later, the referee must write *two* reports, one for each incident.

8 The report must be submitted within two working days.

If the referee is still confused when he comes to complete his first misconduct form, I advise him to contact someone with experience, to check it over and help him to write it if necessary.

Assaults on the referee

Although assaults on referees have become a disturbingly more common problem, they are still, mercifully, rare. Looking at the number of assaults in a recent season, I calculated that statistically a referee is likely to be assaulted only once every 40 seasons. The problem is that when it does occur, the referee may be taken by surprise. If it happens, the referee should follow some simple guidelines.

I Decide whether or not to abandon the game. In general it is advisable to abandon the game immediately following an assault. In the case of serious injury, this may be a very obvious and straightforward decision. Often, however, referees try to carry on and then realise that they are concussed, suffering from double vision, or just very shaken up. If in *any* doubt, the referee is advised to abandon the game, especially if he needs medical attention.

2 Obtain names and addresses of witnesses. This may not always be practicable, but if at all possible the referee should do so because it makes any subsequent civil or criminal action much simpler.

3 Notify the police if actual bodily harm has been done. It is important that the referee does this as quickly as possible so that the police can interview the parties and talk to witnesses.

Unit 4

4 **Report the whole matter to the appropriate authority.** The referee is advised to do this both in writing and by telephone. Normally the player concerned will be suspended immediately, and the secretary of the authority under whose auspices the game is being played will need to be informed quickly so that he can do this.

5 **Inform the Referees' Association local secretary.** Most referees join the Referees' Association, and thus gain the advantage of legal advice and support. Injury suffered and time lost from work may require the referee to sue the player concerned in civil court, and the Referees' Association will help here.

6 **Keep a copy of all correspondence.** This is an essential precaution.

7 **Inform the appropriate authority and Referees' Association local secretary of the result of any prosecution.** Naturally, with the incidence of assault still low, most referees may officiate for many years without being affected. Assault, however, may be totally unexpected. One referee recently suffered a serious assault after asking a spectator to move his young son back a few paces from the line as he was concerned for the small boy's safety. A few years ago, two referees of my acquaintance suffered serious assaults in pre-season 'friendlies'. Forewarned is forearmed!

Answers

A **4.1** The referee should award a penalty kick. A penalty is awarded according to where the *incident* occurred and not where the *ball* was when it happened. The referee should also send the player off as he used excessive force.

A **4.2** Stop play. Both players should be sent off for violent conduct and their actions fully explained on the report forms. The game should be re-started with a dropped ball from where the ball was when the referee stopped the game, unless the ball was in the goal area, when it should be dropped at the nearest point on the edge of the goal area. A penalty kick should not be awarded because the incident occurred off the field of play (i.e. behind the goal line).

A **4.3** This is deliberate handball and the referee should award a penalty kick. Since the player has unfairly stopped an almost certain goal, the Law now requires that he should be sent off for this offence.

Unit 4

A **4.4** No action. The position of the goalkeeper's hands are important here, and provided he handles the ball within the penalty area, he has done nothing wrong.

A **4.5** This represents handball, and the referee should award a direct free kick to the opponents, to be taken from where the ball was handled by the goalkeeper.

A **4.6** No action. The referee should not penalise *unintentional* handball.

A **4.7** No. If the referee considers that the behaviour of the player merits a caution or sending off as appropriate, then he should not hesitate to take action.

A **4.8** The referee should give an indirect free kick *against* the player trying to head the ball. By putting himself in a dangerous position, the player is unfairly distracting the opponent.

A **4.9** No action. Provided the defender who headed the ball has not done so in a deliberate effort to circumvent the laws (by heading it on after it has been deliberately chipped up in the air by a colleague, for example). If an attempt has been made to circumvent the Laws, the offending player should be cautioned and shown the yellow card. If this occurs at the taking of a free kick the player should be dealt with and the free kick re-taken.

A **4.10** (a) If the goalkeeper touches or catches the ball, he should be penalised by the award of an indirect free kick from where the offence occurred. If the offence occurred within the goal area, the free kick should be taken from the nearest point on the edge of the goal area parallel to the goal line. (b) No action.

A **4.11** The goalkeeper can do this for as long as he likes since it is possible for an opponent to legitimately challenge for the ball. It is only when he has taken control of the ball in his hands that he may be accused of time wasting. The referee should point this out to the opponent who is complaining.

A **4.12** The referee should stop the game. Although the player is off the field of play, he should still be dealt with and reported by the referee for violent conduct. The game should be re-started with a dropped ball from where the ball was when play was stopped.

Unit 4

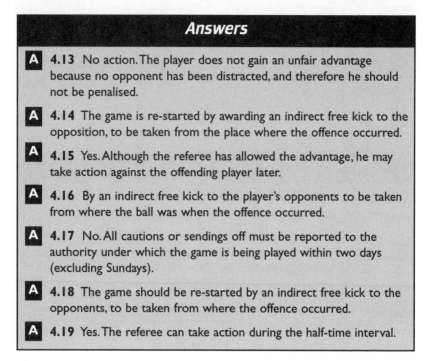

Answers

A **4.13** No action. The player does not gain an unfair advantage because no opponent has been distracted, and therefore he should not be penalised.

A **4.14** The game is re-started by awarding an indirect free kick to the opposition, to be taken from the place where the offence occurred.

A **4.15** Yes. Although the referee has allowed the advantage, he may take action against the offending player later.

A **4.16** By an indirect free kick to the player's opponents to be taken from where the ball was when the offence occurred.

A **4.17** No. All cautions or sendings off must be reported to the authority under which the game is being played within two days (excluding Sundays).

A **4.18** The game should be re-started by an indirect free kick to the opponents, to be taken from where the offence occurred.

A **4.19** Yes. The referee can take action during the half-time interval.

UNIT 5

Free kicks and penalty kicks

PART 1 • Free kicks

During the game the referee will award two types of free kick: direct and indirect. To remind yourself of what we considered in Unit 4, check back on:

• the ten penal offences for which a direct free kick can be awarded
• the offences for which an indirect free kick is awarded.

The difference between a direct and an indirect free kick is that it is possible to score a goal 'directly' against the opposing team from a direct free kick without the ball being touched by another player. If the ball is kicked directly into goal from an indirect free kick, the referee should award a goal kick, or a corner kick if it is kicked by a player into his own goal. It is worth noting here that if a player kicks the ball directly into his own goal from a direct or indirect free kick, the correct decision is still a corner kick.

To ensure that players are aware that the referee has given an indirect free kick, he is required to keep his arm vertically upright at the taking of the kick. Quite frequently players will ask whether a kick is direct or indirect, even when the referee has punished an obvious penal offence such as deliberate handball or a trip. If the kick is near to goal, and awarded to the attacking side, a useful piece of advice is to try to tell the goalkeeper if it is direct or indirect. This is not required by the Laws, but it helps to avoid misunderstandings and subsequent argument, and thus prevents problems occurring when a goal is disputed or claimed.

Refer to the Laws and now answer the following questions.

Unit 5

Questions

(Answers on page 100.)

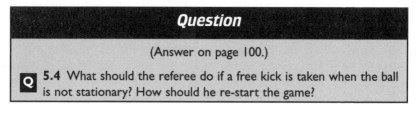

Q 5.1 How long should the referee keep his arm vertical at the taking of an indirect free kick?

Q 5.2 An indirect free kick is awarded. The ball is kicked directly into the opponents' goal. Unfortunately, the referee has failed to raise his arm indicating that the kick is indirect. The scoring team protests because the referee refuses to allow the goal. Is the referee correct in his decision?

Q 5.3 Can a free kick be passed backwards?

The conditions for a correctly taken free kick

The Laws require certain conditions to be met for a free kick to be correctly taken.

(A) The ball must be stationary
A team could gain an unfair advantage if a player was allowed to kick a moving ball at a free kick, since it may be possible to kick it further. Also, because the opposition is expecting the ball to be 'dead' before being kicked, there is likely to be some confusion and it would be unjust to allow the game to continue if this occurs.

Question

(Answer on page 100.)

Q 5.4 What should the referee do if a free kick is taken when the ball is not stationary? How should he re-start the game?

(B) The kick must take place from where the incident occurred
This is, of course, simple common sense. An exception is made, however, if the incident occurred within one team's goal area. If the kick is an indirect one to the attacking side, then it should be taken from the nearest point on the edge of the goal area. If it is a direct or an indirect kick to the defending side, it can be taken from anywhere within the goal area. It is also simple common sense to remember that the referee cannot always be sure *exactly* where every incident occurred. If the free kick is, say, near to the half-way line, then it is less important for it to be taken in the precise place where the offence

occurred than if it was just outside the penalty area and awarded to the attacking side. If it helps to maintain the game's momentum, then it does not matter so much if the ball is a yard or two away from the point at which the incident occurred. It is wise to be stricter with this when the free kick is awarded to the attacking side and is nearer to the opponents' goal.

(C) *Opposing players must be at least 10 yards from the ball*

Opposing players gain a considerable advantage by standing less than 10 yards from the ball. Often, when the attacking side is awarded a kick in these circumstances, the referee will have problems in ensuring that they retreat the full distance and that, having done so, they remain there until the ball is played.

If players encroach within 10 yards they should be cautioned, and this is a useful power available to the referee to ensure that the side taking the free kick is not disadvantaged, and the re-start of the game delayed.

You could decide to pace out 10 yards and then insist that the players, frequently lined up in a 'wall', retreat the full distance. The danger with this approach is that when your back is turned, the attacking side may push the ball forwards a couple of yards. It is not recommended for the referee to turn his back on the ball unless he has an assistant referee who can keep an eye on this for him. Far better to stand over the ball and gesture to the players to move back until satisfied that they are 10 yards from the ball. The Laws now also allow for the assistant referee to become involved and to come on to the field of play to ensure that opponents stand at least 10 yards from the ball. This may not be appropriate, however, if you are using club assistant referees.

Players often want to take a quick free kick. If this is the case, then the referee should allow this to happen. Attackers will want to get the game moving quickly, and thus seek a quick free kick while the defence is still disorganised and confused. Remember that defenders may not have had a chance to retreat the full 10 yards. If the ball hits a defender in these circumstances, the referee should allow play to continue because this is a risk which the attacking side has opted to take.

With a free kick to the attacking side just outside the defending penalty area, both sides will wish to take up appropriate positions. When he is happy that the defending side is at least 10 yards from the ball and everyone is ready, the referee will want to be in a suitable position. Free kicks such as this are known as 'ceremonial free kicks', and the referee should give a good, clear indication that the game can re-start by blowing his whistle hard and clear when he is happy for the game to re-start.

There is one exception to the Law that opponents should be 10 yards from the ball. This is when the attacking side has been awarded an indirect free kick less than 10 yards from the goal. In this case, the defenders can stand less than 10 yards from the ball so long as they are on the goal line between the goal posts.

(D) The referee must signal for the re-start of play

As stated above, the referee should give a clear signal, preferably a blast on his whistle, when re-starting at a ceremonial free kick. If the game has been stopped due to injury, again it is a good idea to re-start with a clear whistle so that there are no misunderstandings about what is happening.

If the free kick is to be taken in the middle of the field of play, or if the team wishes to take a quick free kick, then the use of the whistle may not be necessary. In fact, over-use of the whistle may be distracting and may reduce its impact when it is *really* needed. A whistle may not be needed at all, at other times the referee simply needs to shout 'Play on!' to ensure that the game keeps moving smoothly.

(E) The ball is in play once it is kicked

Questions

(Answers on page 100.)

Q 5.5 The referee has awarded a free kick to the attacking team just 5 yards from the edge of the defending team's penalty area. A defender stands 5 yards behind the ball. Is he allowed to do this?

Q 5.6 A free kick is awarded for a foul just 4 or 5 yards from the touch line. A player wishes to take a quick free kick. The referee signals his approval and the kick is taken. Unfortunately, the player miskicks the ball over the touch line. He appeals for the kick to be re-taken because an opponent was only 2 or 3 yards from the ball. The kicker alleges that he was 'put off' by the close proximity of the opponent. What should be the referee's decision?

Q 5.7 At a free kick, one player strikes another before the ball is kicked. The referee stops the game and sends the offending player off. How should the game be re-started?

Unit 5

(F) The ball must be touched by another player before the kicker touches it a second time

Once the ball is in play – that is, when it has been kicked – the player taking the kick will be penalised if he touches it again before another player makes contact with it. If this occurs, the referee should award an indirect free kick to be taken from where the player made contact with the ball for a second time.

Question

(Answer on page 100.)

Q **5.8** A free kick is awarded. The ball rebounds from the referee, whereupon the player who took the kick plays it for a second time. What action, if any, should the referee take?

Free kicks in the penalty area to the defending side

A free kick may be given inside the penalty area to the defending side. If this happens, there are several conditions which must be adhered to.

The ball has to leave the penalty area before it is in play

If play is stopped due to an infringement *before* the ball has left the penalty area, but after the ball has been kicked, the game must re-start with the original free kick, because the ball is not in play until it has left the area.

Attacking players must be at least 10 yards from the ball at the taking of the kick, and remain outside the penalty area until the ball is in play

If an attacker 'encroaches' by entering the penalty area before the ball has left it, the kick should be re-taken. Of course, if the defending side is able to get the ball upfield into a strong attacking position, and would gain no advantage from a free kick, the referee can apply the advantage clause and simply play on.

If the offence occurs within the goal area, the ball may be placed anywhere in the goal area where the offence occurred

The defender can select the best position in the goal area and take the kick from that point.

89

Unit 5

Q **5.9** At a free kick near the goal, to be taken by the attacking side, the goalkeeper protests to the referee that an opponent is standing on the goal line next to him. May the referee take any action?

Q **5.10** A free kick is awarded to the defending side within its own penalty area. The ball is mis-hit and goes over the goal line – but not into the goal – before it has left the penalty area. What is the referee's decision?

Free kicks struck into a player's own goal

Occasionally, a player will hit a free kick back to his own goalkeeper. Very occasionally, the ball may be kicked too hard, or the goalkeeper may be inattentive or he may slip, with the result that the ball goes into the goal. If this happens, the referee must award a corner kick because the Laws state that a goal cannot be scored directly into a player's own goal from a free kick, direct or indirect.

Question

(Answer on page 100.)

Q **5.11** A defender takes a free kick just outside his own penalty area, and plays the ball back towards the goalkeeper. Unfortunately, he has not noticed that the goalkeeper is lying injured. Realising that the ball is going into the net, the defender chases after it. Just before the ball can enter the goal, the defender reaches it but slices his kick so that the ball goes over the line into the goal. What action should the referee take?

Unit 5

If a defending player commits one of the ten penal offences within the penalty area, when the ball is in play, the attacking side should be awarded a penalty kick.

Question

(Answer on page 100.)

Q **5.12** Which one penal offence is not committed against an opponent?

The award of a penalty kick is often a critical point in a match. Players normally score from such a kick. In a tight game, the referee's decision here is absolutely critical. Perhaps the worst of any referee's memories concern penalties he should have given but did not, and those he gave but should not have. What at first glance appears a straightforward Law is actually rather complicated, and I will take it stage by stage.

The position of players at a penalty kick

Outfield players

The Law requires that, with the exception of the penalty taker and the goalkeeper, all players should be positioned:

- at least 10 yards from the penalty mark
- behind the penalty mark
- outside the penalty area
- on the field of play.

To ensure that players are at least 10 yards from the ball, an arc of 10 yards radius is drawn from the penalty mark, and all players should be outside this arc.

At first it seems odd to insist that players remain on the field of play, but this makes more sense if you consider what an unscrupulous player might do to distract either the goalkeeper or the kicker if he were allowed to walk off before the penalty kick was taken.

The Law demands that the kicker is identified *before* the kick is taken. This prevents 'gamesmanship' from occurring whereby one player carefully puts the ball on the mark, turns his back on it to walk away a few steps and, once outside the area, is passed by a colleague running in at high speed to take the penalty kick. Once the referee is clear as to who is taking the penalty kick, he should tell the goalkeeper so that it is clear to him who he will be facing when the whistle is blown for the kick to be taken.

No other player is allowed to enter the penalty area or move in front of the penalty mark or within 10 yards of the ball until the ball has been kicked. If players do enter or 'encroach' into the penalty area, there are a number of actions the referee must take.

Questions

(Answers on page 100.)

Q **5.13** At the taking of a penalty kick, a defender encroaches before the kick is taken, and a goal is not scored. What action should the referee take?

Q **5.14** At the taking of a penalty, an attacker enters the penalty area before the ball is kicked, and a goal is scored. What action should the referee take?

We can draw up a simple chart to show what the referee should do if offences occur at the taking of the penalty kick.

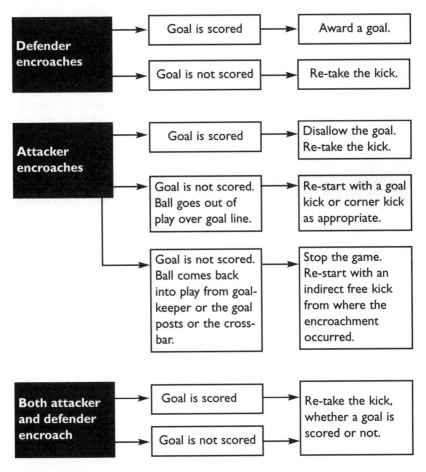

Defender encroaches	Goal is scored	Award a goal.
	Goal is not scored	Re-take the kick.

Attacker encroaches	Goal is scored	Disallow the goal. Re-take the kick.
	Goal is not scored. Ball goes out of play over goal line.	Re-start with a goal kick or corner kick as appropriate.
	Goal is not scored. Ball comes back into play from goal-keeper or the goal posts or the cross-bar.	Stop the game. Re-start with an indirect free kick from where the encroachment occurred.

Both attacker and defender encroach	Goal is scored	Re-take the kick, whether a goal is scored or not.
	Goal is not scored	

The goalkeeper

At the taking of the penalty kick, the defending goalkeeper must stand:

- on his goal line
- facing the kicker
- between the goal posts
- until the ball is kicked.

He is permitted to move his feet before the ball has been kicked, but only along the goal line.

Unit 5

Question

(Answer on page 100.)

Q **5.15** If the goalkeeper moves forwards off his line before the penalty kick has been taken, but after the referee has blown his whistle, what action should the referee take?

A simple chart can help to explain the referee's actions in this case.

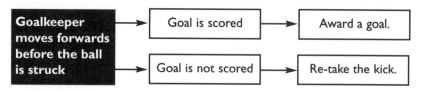

Another offence which can occur here is the penalty taker stopping in his run, encouraging the goalkeeper to move in one direction before the ball is struck. When this happens the kick should be re-taken if a goal is scored, because this behaviour is seen as unsporting and the player concerned must be cautioned.

Questions

(Answers on page 101.)

Q **5.16** Must the ball be played forwards at a penalty kick?

Q **5.17** A penalty kick is awarded. The ground is extremely muddy and slippery. As the kicker runs forwards, he slips and moves the ball forwards about a yard. One of his team-mates then runs in from outside the area and scores. Should the referee award the goal?

Q **5.18** The player taking a penalty kick mis-hits the ball and only manages to kick it forwards a yard or so. He then touches the ball a second time. What action should the referee take?

Outside agents
Very occasionally, something will intrude on to the field of play and will come into contact with the ball. This might include spectators, dogs, overhead wires or even a ball coming on from an adjacent game.

- If the ball comes into contact with such an object on its way towards the goal, re-take the penalty.

- If this happens after the ball rebounds into play from the goal-keeper, or the posts, or the cross-bar, re-start play with a dropped ball from the place where the contact occurred.

Of course, none of these occurrences is very common, but if and when they do occur, it is important to be alert to the action you must take. In particular, remember that you do *not* re-take the penalty kick if the ball hits the spectator, dog, etc. *after* rebounding into play.

A penalty kick in extended time

If a penalty kick is awarded close to the end of a period of play, the referee is instructed to *extend* time for the kick to be taken. Very simply, this means that once the referee has decided whether a goal has been scored, the period is over. Only the kicker and the goal-keeper are therefore involved. Once the outcome of the kick has been resolved, the period of play is over.

The chart on the following page shows what the referee should do when a penalty kick is taken in extended time.

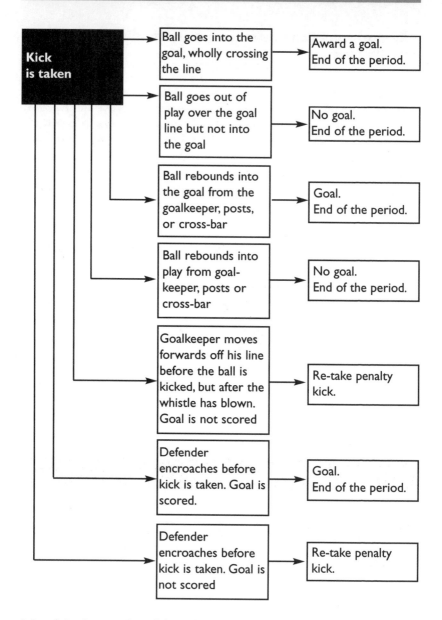

My advice here is that if the referee awards a penalty kick and extends the time for it to be taken, he should inform all the players of what is happening. This avoids the difficulty of explaining why he has stopped the game as soon as the result of the kick is known.

The position of the referee and assistant referees at a penalty kick

You will now appreciate that the referee and his assistants have a great deal to look out for at a penalty kick.

A recommended position was shown in Unit 1, and is reproduced in fig. 41. Here the assistant referee is required to act as a 'goal judge', signalling if a goal is scored, and checking that the goalkeeper does not come off his line before the ball is kicked. As stated earlier, a club assistant referee is unlikely to be asked to do this. The referee judges encroachment and that the kick is correctly taken.

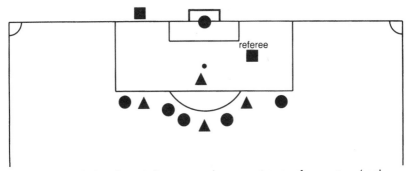

Fig. 41 Penalty kick: referee judges encroachment; assistant referee acts as 'goal judge' and checks for the goalkeeper moving off his line before the ball is kicked

---

Question

(Answer on page 101.)

Q 5.19 A team is awarded a penalty kick during a game. The usual penalty taker is a substitute. May a player of the team be withdrawn and the substitute allowed to go on and take the kick?

Deciding the result of a game by kicks from the penalty mark

It is possible for matches to be decided on kicks from the penalty mark at the end of extra time if the game is still drawn. The Law is now well described in the *Laws of the Game* with a check list to make understanding easier. Fig. 42 shows the position to be taken up by players and officials.

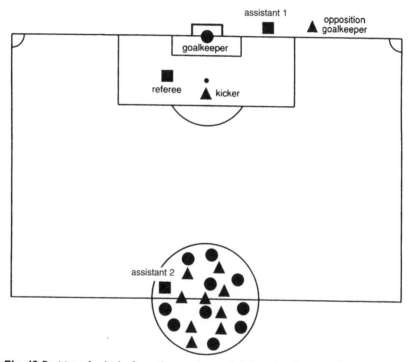

Fig. 42 Positions for kicks from the penalty mark (a 'penalty shoot-out')

Unit 5

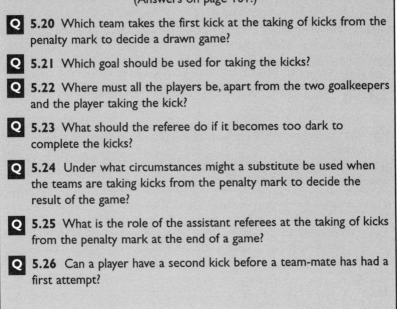

Questions

(Answers on page 101.)

Q **5.20** Which team takes the first kick at the taking of kicks from the penalty mark to decide a drawn game?

Q **5.21** Which goal should be used for taking the kicks?

Q **5.22** Where must all the players be, apart from the two goalkeepers and the player taking the kick?

Q **5.23** What should the referee do if it becomes too dark to complete the kicks?

Q **5.24** Under what circumstances might a substitute be used when the teams are taking kicks from the penalty mark to decide the result of the game?

Q **5.25** What is the role of the assistant referees at the taking of kicks from the penalty mark at the end of a game?

Q **5.26** Can a player have a second kick before a team-mate has had a first attempt?

Matches which are decided on kicks from the penalty mark are becoming more common. However, they do pose a problem for the referee because with the Law being rather complicated, the danger is that he may not be fully aware of the Law. Since the result is at stake, it is important that he gets the details absolutely right. Every time a match could end in this way, it is strongly advisable to read and re-read the procedure beforehand to make absolutely certain that problems will not arise.

Unit 5

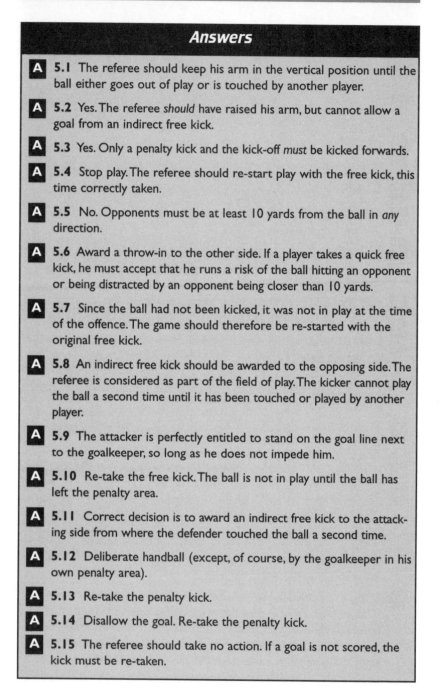

Answers

A **5.1** The referee should keep his arm in the vertical position until the ball either goes out of play or is touched by another player.

A **5.2** Yes. The referee *should* have raised his arm, but cannot allow a goal from an indirect free kick.

A **5.3** Yes. Only a penalty kick and the kick-off *must* be kicked forwards.

A **5.4** Stop play. The referee should re-start play with the free kick, this time correctly taken.

A **5.5** No. Opponents must be at least 10 yards from the ball in *any* direction.

A **5.6** Award a throw-in to the other side. If a player takes a quick free kick, he must accept that he runs a risk of the ball hitting an opponent or being distracted by an opponent being closer than 10 yards.

A **5.7** Since the ball had not been kicked, it was not in play at the time of the offence. The game should therefore be re-started with the original free kick.

A **5.8** An indirect free kick should be awarded to the opposing side. The referee is considered as part of the field of play. The kicker cannot play the ball a second time until it has been touched or played by another player.

A **5.9** The attacker is perfectly entitled to stand on the goal line next to the goalkeeper, so long as he does not impede him.

A **5.10** Re-take the free kick. The ball is not in play until the ball has left the penalty area.

A **5.11** Correct decision is to award an indirect free kick to the attacking side from where the defender touched the ball a second time.

A **5.12** Deliberate handball (except, of course, by the goalkeeper in his own penalty area).

A **5.13** Re-take the penalty kick.

A **5.14** Disallow the goal. Re-take the penalty kick.

A **5.15** The referee should take no action. If a goal is not scored, the kick must be re-taken.

Unit 5

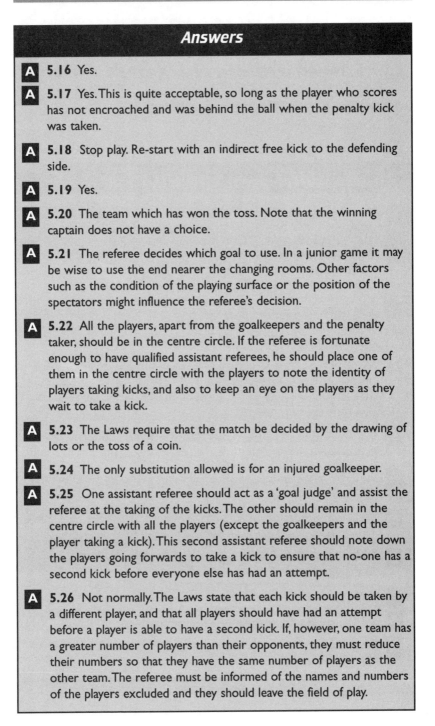

Answers

A **5.16** Yes.

A **5.17** Yes. This is quite acceptable, so long as the player who scores has not encroached and was behind the ball when the penalty kick was taken.

A **5.18** Stop play. Re-start with an indirect free kick to the defending side.

A **5.19** Yes.

A **5.20** The team which has won the toss. Note that the winning captain does not have a choice.

A **5.21** The referee decides which goal to use. In a junior game it may be wise to use the end nearer the changing rooms. Other factors such as the condition of the playing surface or the position of the spectators might influence the referee's decision.

A **5.22** All the players, apart from the goalkeepers and the penalty taker, should be in the centre circle. If the referee is fortunate enough to have qualified assistant referees, he should place one of them in the centre circle with the players to note the identity of players taking kicks, and also to keep an eye on the players as they wait to take a kick.

A **5.23** The Laws require that the match be decided by the drawing of lots or the toss of a coin.

A **5.24** The only substitution allowed is for an injured goalkeeper.

A **5.25** One assistant referee should act as a 'goal judge' and assist the referee at the taking of the kicks. The other should remain in the centre circle with all the players (except the goalkeepers and the player taking a kick). This second assistant referee should note down the players going forwards to take a kick to ensure that no-one has a second kick before everyone else has had an attempt.

A **5.26** Not normally. The Laws state that each kick should be taken by a different player, and that all players should have had an attempt before a player is able to have a second kick. If, however, one team has a greater number of players than their opponents, they must reduce their numbers so that they have the same number of players as the other team. The referee must be informed of the names and numbers of the players excluded and they should leave the field of play.

UNIT 6
The throw-in, goal kick and corner kick

PART 1 • The throw-in

If the whole of the ball passes over the touch line, either on the ground or in the air, a throw-in is awarded to the opposing team to that of the player who last played it. There is a sequence of actions needed for a correctly taken throw-in to occur.

1 The throw-in should be taken from the place where the ball crossed the touch line.
2 Both of the player's feet must remain *on* or *behind* the touch line, as the ball is thrown.
3 The ball should be delivered from behind and over the head.
4 The ball should be *thrown* and not *dropped*, using both hands.
5 The ball must be played by another player before it is played a second time by the thrower.

From the list above it can be seen that the referee and his assistant on that touch line have a great deal to scrutinise. Any offence which results in the ball being incorrectly thrown in, is described as a 'foul throw'. It is penalised by the throw-in being awarded to the other side.

Questions

(Answers on page 108.)

Q 6.1 The player taking the throw-in advances 6 yards up the field from where the ball passed over the touch line before throwing it in. What is the referee's decision?

Q 6.2 The player taking the throw-in retreats 6 yards from where the ball passed over the touch line so that he can throw the ball back to his goalkeeper. What is the referee's decision?

The throw-in should be made from the place where the ball crossed the touch line

Players are loathe to lose the advantage gained from the throw-in by giving away a 'foul throw', with the result that they will often ask the referee where the throw should be taken from. The referee should always guide players to the correct place, and try to warn them first if they are about to throw the ball from the wrong position. He should only give a foul throw for the ball being thrown in from the wrong place if the player has taken the throw too quickly for him to be warned. It is important to make sure that they do not gain an unfair advantage by advancing or retreating along the touch line.

Part of both of the player's feet shall remain on or behind the touch line when the throw is taken

It is important that part of both the player's feet remain on the ground as the throw is being taken. The reason for this is that the player can gain a considerable advantage by throwing the ball much further if he lifts a foot, and most players are aware of this. Often players misunderstand the part of the Law that concerns the position of the feet. If the player's feet are as shown in fig. 43, the throw-in is perfectly legal – part of both feet are on or behind the line. However, remember that if the player raises his heels off the ground as he throws the ball, and the front parts of his feet are inside the field of play, it is a foul throw as he does not have part of both feet *on* or *behind* the line.

Fig. 43 Legal throw-in – part of both feet are on or behind the touch line

The ball shall be thrown from behind and over the head

The player should throw the ball with one hand on either side of the ball as shown below. The action of the throw should start *behind* the head, and the ball should be released after the ball has passed *over* the head.

The ball is sometimes thrown with a one-handed action, giving the thrower an unfair advantage because this puts more power into the throw. It is difficult to spot this, but the tell-tale sign is the fact that the ball spins in the air after it is thrown in this way.

Fig. 44 One hand must be on either side of the ball

The ball must be thrown and not dropped

A thrower may wish to throw the ball to a colleague only a short distance away. To do this, he may choose to drop the ball rather than throw it. This is not allowed, and is penalised by the throw being awarded to the opposition.

The ball enters the field of play

The ball must enter the field of play before it is in play at the taking of a throw-in.

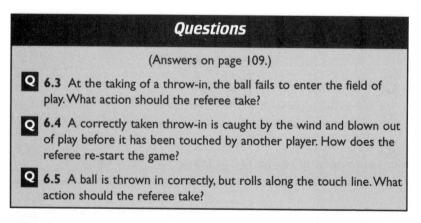

Questions

(Answers on page 109.)

Q 6.3 At the taking of a throw-in, the ball fails to enter the field of play. What action should the referee take?

Q 6.4 A correctly taken throw-in is caught by the wind and blown out of play before it has been touched by another player. How does the referee re-start the game?

Q 6.5 A ball is thrown in correctly, but rolls along the touch line. What action should the referee take?

Unit 6

Questions cont.

Q **6.6** A player takes a throw-in but kicks the ball before it has touched another player. What action should the referee take?

Q **6.7** A player taking a throw-in deliberately handles the ball in the field of play after it has been thrown in, but before it has been touched by another player. What action should the referee take?

Throwing the ball to the goalkeeper

When a throw-in is taken, the ball may be thrown back to the goalkeeper of the thrower's team. When this happens, the goalkeeper cannot pick up the ball with his hands but can only play the ball with his feet. If he picks up the ball an indirect free kick should be awarded against him, to be taken from where he made contact with the ball.

When watching a throw-in, the referee and his assistants will often look at different aspects. For example, the referee might instruct the assistants to look at the thrower's feet while he concentrates on the hands. The assistant referee will signal any fault observed to the referee so that the throw-in can be awarded to the other side.

The ball may be seen by the referee to clearly go out of play, but he may be unaware of who last touched it. A clear signal from the assistant referee is important here to indicate which side is entitled to the throw. There are times when the referee has clearly seen who last kicked the ball, but is unsure of whether it has wholly gone out of play. The assistant, being in a better position to judge this, can give a good signal to the referee to show him that a throw-in should be awarded.

A clear understanding between the three officials is important. Concentration and teamwork can ensure that errors are minimised.

Other aspects of the throw-in need to be considered . . .

Questions

(Answers on page 109.)

Q **6.8** Can a goalkeeper take a throw-in?

Q **6.9** When a throw-in is being taken, an opponent jumps up and down in front of the thrower. What action should the referee take?

Q **6.10** What should the referee's decision be if the ball is thrown by a player directly into: (a) his opponents' goal; (b) his own goal?

Unit 6

Questions cont.

Q **6.11** This is a situation experienced by a colleague in a game recently, and which caused some argument among referees. A throw-in was awarded to the defending team about 15 yards from its goal line. A defender threw the ball back to his goalkeeper but failed to notice a forward, who ran quickly between him and the goalkeeper and intercepted the ball. The forward kicked the ball into the goal. The referee turned to see the assistant referee flag for a foul throw. What action should the referee have taken?

PART 2 • The goal kick

If the whole of the ball passes over the goal line, either on the ground or in the air, and a goal is not legitimately scored, having been last touched by an attacking player, the referee must award a goal kick.

The procedure for a correctly taken goal kick is as follows:

The ball can be placed anywhere in the goal area
In an effort to speed the game up, goal kicks may now be taken from anywhere in the goal area.

The ball must leave the penalty area before it is in play
This can be shown by considering the following questions:

Questions

(Answers on page 109.)

Q **6.12** A goal kick is taken. Before the ball has left the penalty area, the referee sees a player strike an opponent. What action should the referee take?

Q **6.13** A goal kick is accidentally kicked over the goal line before it has left the penalty area. What action should the referee take?

It is a valuable aid to the referee if the assistant referee observes carefully the taking of a goal kick to ensure that the ball leaves the penalty area before it is touched by another player. If, for example, the ball comes to the edge of the penalty area and is then passed back

Unit 6

to the goalkeeper by a defender before it has left the area, the referee must stop play and order the kick to be re-taken.

Attacking players must not enter the penalty area until the ball has passed out of it
Often a goalkeeper will take a short goal kick, passing the ball to a colleague just outside the penalty area. An attacker seeing this might run across the area to intercept the ball or challenge the defender. This is not allowed. The referee should insist that the kick is re-taken, and advise the attacker about this breach of the Law.

Two other aspects of the goal kick you need to be aware of are:

1 A goal can be scored direct from a goal kick.
2 A player cannot be offside if he receives the ball direct from a goal kick.

Many players, even at senior level, are unaware that it is impossible to be offside from a goal kick. This can result in some controversy if a goal is scored following such a move. A team I once played for used this as a tactic in the game. We had a strong centre-half who could kick the ball upfield into the opponents' half. Our centre-forward would stand about 15 yards 'offside', collect the ball and run for goal. Frequently, the opposition would besiege the referee demanding to know why offside had not been given. Meanwhile, my side would be waiting to re-start the game.

Question

(Answer on page 109.)

Q 6.14 On what occasions can the ball pass into the goal and a goal kick be awarded?

PART 3 • The corner kick

If the ball passes wholly over the goal line, either on the ground or in the air, and a goal is not legitimately scored, having been last touched by a defender, the referee must award a corner kick. A corner kick must be taken from the quadrant at the corner of the field closest to where the ball crossed the goal line. When a corner kick is awarded, the following conditions must apply:

Unit 6

The ball is in play as soon as it is kicked
This is a standard condition for all re-starts of play which involve a kick, except a dropped ball.

Opponents must be positioned at least 10 yards from the ball
Until the ball is kicked, opponents must be at least 10 yards away. If they encroach, the referee should order the kick to be re-taken, unless there is no advantage to the attacking side in doing so.

The player taking the kick must not play the ball a second time until it has been played or touched by another player
Again, this is a normal condition.

Question

(Answer on page 109.)

Q 6.15 The ball rebounds from the goal post at a corner kick to the player who originally took the kick, who touches it a second time. What action should the referee take?

It is worth remembering that it is impossible to be judged offside directly from a corner kick.

There is one other aspect of the corner kick to consider . . .

Question

(Answer on page 109.)

Q 6.16 Can a goal be scored directly from a corner kick?

Answers

A 6.1 Foul throw since the ball must be thrown in from the point where it crossed the line. Award the throw-in to the other side. Always try to advise the player about the correct place before he throws it, if this is practicable.

A 6.2 Foul throw, for the reasons stated directly above. Players cannot advance or retreat from the correct position when taking a throw-in.

Unit 6

A **6.3** Order a re-take of the throw-in. The ball is not in play until part of it has entered the field of play.

A **6.4** Award a throw-in to the other side, to be taken from where the ball left the field of play following the throw-in.

A **6.5** Play on. The markings are part of the field of play.

A **6.6** Award an indirect free kick to the opposition to be taken from where the player kicked the ball. The ball must not be played by the thrower until it has been touched by another player.

A **6.7** Award a direct free kick. The ball has been handled deliberately. The more serious offence is penalised.

A **6.8** Yes. There is no reason why the goalkeeper cannot take a throw-in.

A **6.9** Delay the throw-in. Caution the opponent for unsporting behaviour.

A **6.10** (a) Goal kick; (b) corner kick.

A **6.11** The referee should have the throw-in awarded to the other team, as this is a foul throw. It is not possible to play the advantage from a foul throw.

A **6.12** The referee should stop the game and send off the culprit for violent conduct. The game must be re-started with the goal kick because the ball was not in play at the time of the offence as it had not left the penalty area.

A **6.13** Re-take the goal kick. Again, the ball has not left the penalty area and is thus not in play.

A **6.14** When it goes into the goal direct from an indirect free kick or a throw-in taken by the attacking side.

A **6.15** Award an indirect free kick from the place where the kicker made contact with the ball for a second time. The ball must be played or touched by a second player before the kicker may play it again.

A **6.16** Yes, but only in the opponents' goal.

LAWS OF THE GAME

The following Laws were first published in July 2000 by FIFA and are authorised by the International Football Association Board.

Notes on the Laws of the Game

Modifications
Subject to the agreement of the national association concerned and provided the principles of these Laws are maintained, the Laws may be modified in their application for matches for players of under 16 years of age, for women footballers and for veteran footballers (over 35 years).

Any or all of the following modifications are permissible:

* *size of the field of play*
* *size, weight and material of the ball*
* *width between the goalposts and height of the crossbar from the ground*
* *the duration of the periods of play*
* *substitutions.*

Further modifications are only allowed with the consent of the International Football Association Board.

Male and Female
References to the male gender in the Laws of the Game in respect of referees, assistant referees, players and officials are for simplification and apply to both males and females.

Key

Throughout the Laws of the Game the following symbols are used:

* Unless covered by the Special Circumstances listed in Law 8 – The Start and Restart of Play

| Single line indicates new Law changes [changes for 2000/1]

Laws of the Game

Contents

1	THE FIELD OF PLAY	112
2	THE BALL	114
3	THE NUMBER OF PLAYERS	115
4	THE PLAYERS' EQUIPMENT	116
5	THE REFEREE	117
6	THE ASSISTANT REFEREES	119
7	THE DURATION OF THE MATCH	120
8	THE START AND RESTART OF PLAY	121
9	THE BALL IN AND OUT OF PLAY	122
10	THE METHOD OF SCORING	122
11	OFFSIDE	123
12	FOULS AND MISCONDUCT	123
13	FREE KICKS	125
14	THE PENALTY KICK	127
15	THE THROW-IN	128
16	THE GOAL KICK	130
17	THE CORNER KICK	131
	KICKS FROM THE PENALTY MARK	132
	THE TECHNICAL AREA	133
	THE FOURTH OFFICIAL	133

Laws of the Game

LAW I – The Field of Play

Dimensions
The field of play must be rectangular. The length of the touch line must be greater than the length of the goal line.

Length: minimum 90 m (100 yds)
         maximum 120 m (130 yds)
Width: minimum 45 m (50 yds)
         maximum 90 m (100 yds)

International Matches

Length: minimum 100 m (110 yds)
         maximum 110 m (120 yds)
Width: minimum 64m (70 yds)
         maximum 75 m (80 yds)

Field Markings
The field of play is marked with lines. These lines belong to the areas of which they are boundaries.

The two longer boundary lines are called touch lines. The two shorter lines are called goal lines.

All lines are not more than 12 cm (5 ins) wide.

The field of play is divided into two halves by a halfway line.

The centre mark is indicated at the midpoint of the halfway line. A circle with a radius of 9.15 m (10 yds) is marked around it.

The Goal Area
A goal area is defined at each end of the field as follows:

Two lines are drawn at right angles to the goal line, 5.5 m (6 yds) from the inside of the goalpost. These lines extend into the field of play for a distance of 5.5 m (6 yds) and are joined by a line drawn parallel with the goal line. The area bounded by these lines and the goal line is the goal area.

The Penalty Area
A penalty area is defined at each end of the field as follows:

Two lines are drawn at right angles to the goal line, 16.5 m (18 yds) from the inside of each goalpost. These lines extend into the field of play for a distance of 16.5 m (18 yds) and are joined by a line drawn parallel with the goal line. The area bounded by these lines and the goal line is the penalty area.

Within each penalty area a penalty mark is made 11 m (12 yds) from the midpoint between the goalposts and equidistant to them. An arc of a circle with a radius of 9.15 m (10 yds) is drawn outside the penalty area.

Flagposts
A flagpost, not less than 1.5 m (5 ft) high, with a non-pointed top and a flag is placed at each corner.

Flagposts may also be placed at each end of the halfway line, not less than 1 m (1 yd) outside the touch line.

The Corner Arc
A quarter circle with a radius of 1 m (1 yd) from each corner flagpost is drawn inside the field of play.

Goals
Goals must be placed on the centre of each goal line.

They consist of two upright posts equidistant from the corner flagposts and joined at the top by a horizontal crossbar.

The distance between the posts is 7.32 m (8 yds) and the distance from the lower edge of the crossbar to the ground is 2.44 m (8 ft).

Laws of the Game

Both goalposts and the crossbar have the same width and depth which do not exceed 12 cm (5 ins). The goal lines are the same width as that of the goalposts and the crossbar. Nets may be attached to the goals and the ground behind the goal, provided that they are properly supported and do not interfere with the goalkeeper.

The goalposts and crossbars must be white.

Safety
Goals must be anchored securely to the ground. Portable goals may only be used if they satisfy this requirement.

Decisions of the International F.A. Board

• Decision 1
If the crossbar becomes displaced or broken, play is stopped until it has been repaired or replaced in position. If a repair is not possible, the match is abandoned. The use of a rope to replace the crossbar is not permitted. If the crossbar can be repaired, the match is restarted with a dropped ball at the place where the ball was located when play was stopped. *[see page 110]

• Decision 2
Goalposts and crossbars must be made of wood, metal or other approved material. Their shape may be square, rectangular, round or elliptical and they must not be dangerous to players.

• Decision 3
No kind of commercial advertising, whether real or virtual, is permitted on the field of play and field equipment (including the goal nets and the areas they enclose) from the time the teams enter the field of play until they have left it at half time and from the time the teams re-enter the field of play until the end of the match. In particular, no advertising material of any kind may be displayed on goals, nets, flagposts or

their flags. No extraneous equipment (cameras, microphones, etc.) may be attached to these items.

• Decision 4
There shall be no advertising of any kind within the technical area or within one metre from the touch line and outside the field of play on the ground. Further, no advertising shall be allowed in the area between the goal line and the goal nets.

• Decision 5
The reproduction, whether real or virtual, of representative logos or emblems of FIFA, confederations, national associations, leagues, clubs or other bodies, is forbidden on the field of play and field equipment (including the goal nets and the areas they enclose) during playing time, as described in Decision 3.

• Decision 6
A mark may be made off the field of play, 9.15 metres (10 yds) from the corner arc and at right angles to the goal line, to ensure that this distance is observed when a corner kick is being taken.

LAW 2 – The Ball

Qualities and Measurements

The ball is:

• *spherical*

• *made of leather or other suitable material*

• *of a circumference of not more than 70 cm (28 ins) and not less than 68 cm (27 ins)*

• *not more than 450 g (16 oz) in weight and not less than 410 g (14 oz) at the start of the match*

• *of a pressure equal to 0.6–1.1 atmosphere (600–1100 g/cm^2) above atmospheric pressure at sea level (8.5 lbs/sq. in–15.6 lbs/sq. in)*

Replacement of a Defective Ball

If the ball bursts or becomes defective during the course of a match:

• *the match is stopped*

• *it is restarted by dropping the replacement ball at the place where the first ball became defective *[see page 110]*

If the ball bursts or becomes defective whilst not in play at a kick off, goal kick, corner kick, free kick, penalty kick or throw-in:

• *the match is restarted accordingly*

The ball may not be changed during the match without the authority of the referee.

Decisions of the International F.A. Board

• Decision 1
In competition matches, only footballs which meet the minimum technical requirements stipulated in Law 2 are permitted for use.

In FIFA competition matches and in competition matches organised under the auspices of the confederations, acceptance of a football for use is conditional upon the football bearing one of the following three designations:

the official "FIFA APPROVED" logo, or
the official "FIFA INSPECTED" logo, or
the reference "INTERNATIONAL MATCHBALL STANDARD"

Such a designation on a football indicates that it has been tested officially and found to be in compliance with specific technical requirements, different for each category and additional to the minimum specifications stipulated in Law 2. The list of the additional requirements specific to each of the respective categories must be approved by the International F.A. Board. The institutes conducting the tests are subject to the approval of FIFA.

National association competitions may require the use of balls bearing any one of these three designations.

In all other matches the ball used must satisfy the requirements of Law 2.

• Decision 2
In FIFA competition matches, and in competition matches organised under the auspices of the confederations and national associations, no kind of commercial advertising is permitted on the ball, except for the emblem of the competition, the competition organiser and the authorised trademark of the manufacturer. The competition regulations may restrict the size and number of such markings.

Laws of the Game

LAW 3 – The Number of Players

Players

A match is played by two teams, each consisting of not more than eleven players, one of whom is the goalkeeper. A match may not start if either team consists of fewer than seven players.

Official Competitions

Up to a maximum of three substitutes may be used in any match played in an official competition under the auspices of FIFA, the confederations or the national associations.

The rules of the competition must state how many substitutes may be nominated, from three up to a maximum of seven.

Other Matches

In other matches, substitutes may be used provided that:

• *the teams concerned reach agreement on a maximum number*

• *the referee is informed before the match*

If the referee is not informed, or if no agreement is reached before the start of the match, no more than three substitutes are allowed.

All Matches

In all matches the names of the substitutes must be given to the referee prior to the start of the match. Substitutes not so named may not take part in the match.

Substitution Procedure

To replace a player by a substitute, the following conditions must be observed:

• *the referee is informed before any proposed substitution is made*

• *a substitute only enters the field of play after the player being replaced has left and after receiving a signal from the referee*

• *a substitute only enters the field of play at the halfway line and during a stoppage in the match*

• *a substitution is completed when a substitute enters the field of play*

• *from that moment, the substitute becomes a player and the player he has replaced ceases to be a player*

• *a player who has been replaced takes no further part in the match*

• *all substitutes are subject to the authority and jurisdiction of the referee, whether called upon to play or not*

Changing the Goalkeeper

Any of the other players may change places with the goalkeeper, provided that:

• *the referee is informed before the change is made*

• *the change is made during a stoppage in the match*

Infringements/Sanctions

If a substitute enters the field of play without the referee being informed:

• *play is stopped*

• *the substitute is cautioned, shown the yellow card and required to leave the field of play*

• *play is restarted with a dropped ball at the place it was located when play was stopped *[see page 110]*

If a player changes places with a goalkeeper without the referee being informed before the change is made:

• *play continues*

• *the players concerned are cautioned and shown the yellow card when the ball is next out of play*

For any other infringements of this Law:

• *the players concerned are cautioned and shown the yellow card*

Restart of play
If play is stopped by the referee to administer a caution:

• *the match is restarted by an indirect free kick, to be taken by a player of the opposing team from the place where*

the ball was when play was stopped *[see page 110]

Players and Substitutes Sent Off
A player who has been sent off before the kick-off may be replaced only by one of the named substitutes.

A named substitute who has been sent off, either before the kick-off or after play has started, may not be replaced.

Decisions of the International F.A. Board

• Decision I
Subject to the overriding conditions of Law 3, the minimum number of players in a team is left to the discretion of national associations. The Board is of the opinion, however, that a match should not continue if there are fewer than seven players in either team.

• Decision 2
The coach may convey tactical instructions to the players during the match and he must return to his position immediately after giving these instructions. He and the other officials must remain within the confines of the technical area, where such an area is provided, and they must behave in a responsible manner.

LAW 4 – The Players' Equipment

Safety
A player must not use equipment or wear anything which is dangerous to himself or another player (including any kind of jewellery).

Basic Equipment
The basic compulsory equipment of a player is:

• *a jersey or shirt*

• *shorts – if thermal undershorts are worn, they are of the same main colour as the shorts*

• *stockings*

• *shinguards*

• *footwear*

Shinguards

• *are covered entirely by the stockings*

• *are made of a suitable material (rubber, plastic, or similar substances)*

• *provide a reasonable degree of protection*

Goalkeepers

• *each goalkeeper wears colours which distinguish him from the other players, the referee and the assistant referees*

Infringements/Sanctions

For any infringement of this Law:

• *play need not be stopped*

• the player at fault is instructed by the referee to leave the field of play to correct his equipment

• the player leaves the field of play when the ball next ceases to be in play, unless he has already corrected his equipment

• any player required to leave the field of play to correct his equipment does not re-enter without the permission of the referee

• the referee checks that the player's equipment is correct before allowing him to re-enter the field of play

• the player is only allowed to re-enter the field of play when the ball is out of play

A player who has been required to leave the field of play because of an infringement of this Law and who enters (or re-enters) the field of play without the permission of the referee is cautioned and shown the yellow card.

Restart of Play
If play is stopped by the referee to administer a caution:

• the match is restarted by an indirect free kick taken by a player of the opposing side, from the place where the ball was located when the referee stopped the match *[see page 110]

LAW 5 – The Referee

The Authority of the Referee
Each match is controlled by a referee who has full authority to enforce the Laws of the Game in connection with the match to which he has been appointed.

Powers and Duties

The Referee:

• enforces the Laws of the Game

• controls the match in co-operation with the assistant referees and, where applicable, with the fourth official

• ensures that the ball meets the requirements of Law 2

• ensures that the players' equipment meets the requirements of Law 4

• acts as timekeeper and keeps a record of the match

• stops, suspends or terminates the match, at his discretion, for any infringements of the Laws

• stops, suspends or terminates the match because of outside interference of any kind

• stops the match if, in his opinion, a player is seriously injured and ensures that he is removed from the field of play

• allows play to continue until the ball is out of play if a player is, in his opinion, only slightly injured

• ensures that any player bleeding from a wound leaves the field of play. The player may only return on receiving a signal from the referee, who must be satisfied that the bleeding has stopped

• allows play to continue when the team against which an offence has been committed will benefit from such an advantage and penalises the original offence if the anticipated advantage does not ensue at that time

• punishes the more serious offence when a player commits more than one offence at the same time

• takes disciplinary action against players guilty of cautionable and sending-off offences. He is not obliged to take this action immediately but must do so when the ball next goes out of play

• takes action against team officials who fail to conduct themselves in a responsible manner and may at his discretion, expel them from the field of play and its immediate surrounds

• acts on the advice of assistant referees regarding incidents which he has not seen

• ensures that no unauthorised persons enter the field of play

• restarts the match after it has been stopped

• provides the appropriate authorities with a match report which includes information on any disciplinary action taken against players, and/or team officials and any other incidents which occurred before, during or after the match

Decisions of the Referee

The decisions of the referee regarding facts connected with play are final.

The referee may only change a decision on realising that it is incorrect or, at his discretion, on the advice of an assistant referee, provided that he has not restarted play.

Laws of the Game

Decisions of the International F.A. Board

• Decision I

A referee (or where applicable, an assistant referee or fourth official) is not held liable for:

• any kind of injury suffered by a player, official or spectator

• any damage to property of any kind

• any other loss suffered by any individual, club, company, association or other body, which is due or which may be due to any decision which he may take under the terms of the Laws of the Game or in respect of the normal procedures required to hold, play and control a match.

This may include:

• *a decision that the condition of the field of play or its surrounds or that the weather conditions are such as to allow or not to allow a match to take place*

• *a decision to abandon a match for whatever reason*

• *a decision as to the condition of the fixtures or equipment used during a match including the goalposts, crossbar, flagposts and the ball*

• *a decision to stop or not to stop a match due to spectator interference or any problem in the spectator area*

• *a decision to stop or not to stop play to allow an injured player to be removed from the field of play for treatment*

• *a decision to request or insist that an injured player be removed from the field of play for treatment*

• *a decision to allow or not to allow a player to wear certain apparel or equipment*

• *a decision (in so far as this may be his responsibility) to allow or not to allow any persons (including team or stadium officials, security officers, photographers or other media representatives) to be present in the vicinity of the field of play*

• *any other decision which he may take in accordance with the Laws of the Game or in conformity with his duties under the terms of FIFA, confederation, national association or league rules or regulations under which the match is played*

• Decision 2

In tournaments or competitions where a fourth official is appointed, his role and duties must be in accordance with the guidelines approved by the International F.A. Board.

• Decision 3

Facts connected with play shall include whether a goal is scored or not and the result of the match.

LAW 6 – The Assistant Referees

Duties

Two assistant referees are appointed whose duties, subject to the decision of the referee, are to indicate:

• *when the whole of the ball has passed out of the field of play*

• *which side is entitled to a corner kick, goal kick or throw-in*

• *when a player may be penalised for being in an offside position*

• *when a substitution is requested*

• *when misconduct or any other incident has occurred out of the view of the referee*

• *when offences have been committed whenever the assistants are closer to the action than the referee (this includes, in particular circumstances, offences committed in the penalty area)*

• *whether, at penalty kicks, the goalkeeper has moved forward before the ball has been kicked and if the ball has crossed the line*

Assistance
The assistant referees also assist the referee to control the match in accordance with the Laws of the Game. In paricular, they may enter the field of play to help control the 9.15 m distance.

In the event of undue interference or improper conduct, the referee will relieve an assistant referee of his duties and make a report to the appropriate authorities.

LAW 7 – The Duration of the Match

Periods of Play
The match lasts two equal periods of 45 minutes, unless otherwise mutually agreed between the referee and the two participating teams. Any agreement to alter the periods of play (for example to reduce each half to 40 minutes because of insufficient light) must be made before the start of play and must comply with competition rules.

Half-Time Interval
Players are entitled to an interval at half-time.

The half-time interval must not exceed 15 minutes.

Competition rules must state the duration of the half-time interval.

The duration of the half-time interval may be altered only with the consent of the referee.

Allowance for Time Lost
Allowance is made in either period for all time lost through:

• *substitution(s)*

• *assessment of injury to players*

• *removal of injured players from the field of play for treatment*

• *wasting time*

• *any other cause*

The allowance for time lost is at the discretion of the referee.

Penalty Kick
Additional time is allowed for a penalty kick to be taken at the end of each half or at the end of periods of extra time.

Extra Time
Competition rules may provide for two further equal periods to be played. The conditions of Law 8 will apply.

Abandoned Match
An abandoned match is replayed unless the competition rules provide otherwise.

Laws of the Game

LAW 8 – The Start and Restart of Play

Preliminaries

A coin is tossed and the team which wins the toss decides which goal it will attack in the first half of the match.

The other team takes the kick-off to start the match.

The team which wins the toss takes the kick-off to start the second half of the match.

In the second half of the match the teams change ends and attack the opposite goals.

Kick-off

A kick-off is a way of starting or restarting play:

• *at the start of the match*

• *after a goal has been scored*

• *at the start of the second half of the match*

• *at the start of each period of extra time where applicable*

A goal may be scored directly from the kick-off.

Procedure

• *all players are in their own half of the field*

• *the opponents of the team taking the kick-off are at least 9.15 m (10 yds) from the ball until it is in play*

• *the ball is stationary on the centre mark*

• *the referee gives a signal*

• *the ball is in play when it is kicked and moves forward*

• *the kicker does not touch the ball a second time until it has touched another player*

After a team scores a goal, the kick-off is taken by the other team.

Infringements/Sanctions

If the kicker touches the ball a second time before it has touched another player:

• *an indirect free kick is awarded to the opposing team to be taken from the place where the infringement occurred** [see page 110]

For any other infringement of the kick-off procedure:

• *the kick-off is retaken*

Dropped Ball

A dropped ball is a way of restarting the match after a temporary stoppage which becomes necessary, while the ball is in play, for any reason not mentioned elsewhere in the Laws of the Game.

Procedure

The referee drops the ball at the place where it was located when play was stopped.*[see page 110]

Play restarts when the ball touches the ground.

Infringements/Sanctions

The ball is dropped again:

• *if it is touched by a player before it makes contact with the ground*

or

• *if the ball leaves the field of play after it makes contact with the ground, without a player touching it*

Laws of the Game

Special Circumstances

A free kick awarded to the defending team inside its own goal area is taken from any point within the goal area.

An indirect free kick awarded to the attacking team in its opponents' goal area is taken from the goal area line parallel to the goal line at the point nearest to where the infringement occurred.

A dropped ball to restart the match after play has been temporarily stopped inside the goal area takes place on the goal area line parallel to the goal line at the point nearest to where the ball was located when play was stopped.

LAW 9 – The Ball In and Out of Play

Ball Out of Play

The ball is out of play when:

• *it has wholly crossed the goal line or touch line whether on the ground or in the air*

• *play has been stopped by the referee*

Ball In Play

The ball is in play at all other times, including when:

• *it rebounds from a goalpost, crossbar or corner flagpost and remains in the field of play*

• *it rebounds from either the referee or an assistant referee when they are on the field of play*

LAW 10 – The Method of Scoring

Goal Scored

A goal is scored when the whole of the ball passes over the goal line, between the goalposts and under the crossbar, provided that no infringement of the Laws of the Game has been committed previously by the team scoring the goal.

Winning Team

The team scoring the greater number of goals during a match is the winner. If both teams score an equal number of goals, or if no goals are scored, the match is drawn.

Competition Rules

For matches ending in a draw, competition rules may state provisions involving extra time, or other procedures approved by the International F.A. Board to determine the winner of a match.

Laws of the Game

LAW 11 – Offside

Offside Position

It is not an offence in itself to be in an offside position.

A player is in an offside position if:

• *he is nearer to his opponent's goal line than both the ball and the second last opponent*

A player is not in an offside position if:

• *he is in his own half of the field of play*
or
• *he is level with the second last opponent*
or
• *he is level with the last two opponents*

Offence

A player in an offside position is only penalised if, at the moment the ball touches or is played by one of his team, he is, in the opinion of the referee, involved in active play by:

• *interfering with play*
or
• *interfering with an opponent*
or
• *gaining an advantage by being in that position*

No offence

There is no offside offence if a player receives the ball directly from:

• *a goal kick*
or
• *a throw-in*
or
• *a corner kick*

Infringements/Sanctions

For any offside offence, the referee awards an indirect free kick to the opposing team to be taken from the place where the infringement occurred.
*[see page 110]

LAW 12 – Fouls and Misconduct

Fouls and misconduct are penalised as follows:

Direct Free Kick

A direct free kick is awarded to the opposing team if a player commits any of the following six offences in a manner considered by the referee to be careless, reckless or using excessive force:

• *kicks or attempts to kick an opponent*

• *trips or attempts to trip an opponent*

• *jumps at an opponent*

• *charges an opponent*

• *strikes or attempts to strike an opponent*

• *pushes an opponent*

A direct free kick is also awarded to the opposing team if a player commits any of the following four offences:

• *tackles an opponent to gain possession of the ball, making contact with the opponent before touching the ball*

• *holds an opponent*

• *spits at an opponent*

• *handles the ball deliberately (except for the goalkeeper within his own penalty area)*

Laws of the Game

A direct free kick is taken from where the offence occurred. *[see page 110]

Penalty Kick

A penalty kick is awarded if any of these ten offences is committed by a player inside his own penalty area, irrespective of the position of the ball, provided it is in play.

Indirect Free Kick

An indirect free kick is awarded to the opposing team if a goalkeeper, inside his own penalty area, commits any of the following five offences:

- *takes more than six seconds while controlling the ball with his hands before releasing it from his possession*

- *touches the ball again with his hands after it has been released from his possession and has not touched any other player*

- *touches the ball with his hands after it has been deliberately kicked to him by a team-mate*

- *touches the ball with his hands after he has received it directly from a throw-in taken by a team-mate*

- *wastes time*

An indirect free kick is awarded to the opposing team if a player, in the opinion of the referee:

- *plays in a dangerous manner*

- *impedes the progress of an opponent*

- *prevents the goalkeeper from releasing the ball from his hands*

- *commits any other offence, not previously mentioned in Law 12, for which play is stopped to caution or dismiss a player*

The indirect free kick is taken from where the offence occurred.* [see page 110]

Disciplinary Sanctions

Cautionable Offences

A player is cautioned and shown the yellow card if he commits any of the following seven offences:

1. is guilty of unsporting behaviour

2. shows dissent by word or action

3. persistently infringes the Laws of the Game

4. delays the restart of play

5. fails to respect the required distance when play is restarted with a corner kick or free kick

6. enters or re-enters the field of play without the permission of the referee

7. deliberately leaves the field of play without the permission of the referee

Sending Off Offences

A player is sent off and shown the red card if he commits any of the following seven offences:

1. is guilty of serious foul play

2. is guilty of violent conduct

3. spits at an opponent or any other person

4. denies an opposing team a goal or an obvious goal-scoring opportunity by deliberately handling the ball (this does not apply to a goalkeeper within his own penalty area)

5. denies an obvious goal-scoring opportunity to an opponent moving towards the player's goal by an offence punishable by a free kick or a penalty kick

6. uses offensive or insulting or abusive language and/or gestures

7. receives a second caution in the same match

Laws of the Game

Decisions of the International F.A. Board

• Decision 1

A penalty kick is awarded if, while the ball is in play, the goalkeeper, inside his own penalty area, strikes an opponent by throwing the ball at him.

• Decision 2

A player who commits a cautionable or sending off offence, either on or off the field of play, whether directed towards an opponent, a team mate, the referee, an assistant referee or any other person, is disciplined according to the nature of the offence committed.

• Decision 3

The goalkeeper is considered to be in control of the ball by touching it with any part of his hand or arms. Possession of the ball includes the goalkeeper deliberately parrying the ball, but does not include the circumstances where, in the opinion of the referee, the ball rebounds accidentally from the goalkeeper, for example after he has made a save.

The goalkeeper is considered to be guilty of time-wasting if he holds the ball in his hands or arms for more than 5–6 seconds.

• Decision 4

Subject to the terms of Law 12, a player may pass the ball to his own goalkeeper using his head or chest or knee, etc. If, however, in the opinion of the referee, a player uses a deliberate trick while the ball is in play in order to circumvent the Law, the player is guilty of unsporting behaviour. He is cautioned, shown the yellow card and an indirect free kick is awarded to the opposing team from the place where the infringement occurred.* [see page 110]

A player using a deliberate trick to circumvent the Law while he is taking a free kick, is cautioned for unsporting behaviour and shown the yellow card. The free kick is retaken.

In such circumstances, it is irrelevant whether the goalkeeper subsequently touches the ball with his hands or not. The offence is committed by the player in attempting to circumvent both the letter and the spirit of Law 12.

• Decision 5

A tackle from behind, which endangers the safety of an opponent, must be sanctioned as serious foul play.

• Decision 6

Any stimulating action anywhere on the field, which is intended to deceive the referee, must be sanctioned as unsporting behaviour.

LAW 13 – Free Kicks

Types of Free Kicks

Free kicks are either direct or indirect.

For both direct and indirect free kicks, the ball must be stationary when the kick is taken and the kicker does not touch the ball a second time until it has touched another player.

The Direct Free Kick

• *if a direct free kick is kicked directly into the opponents' goal, a goal is awarded*

• *if a direct free kick is kicked directly into the team's own goal, after the ball is in play, a corner kick is awarded to the opposing team*

The Indirect Free Kick

Signal

The referee indicates an indirect free kick by raising his arm above his head. He maintains his arm in that position until the kick has been taken and the ball has touched another player or goes out of play.

Ball Enters the Goal

A goal can be scored only if the ball subsequently touches another player before it enters the goal.

• *if an indirect free kick is kicked directly into the opponents' goal, a goal kick is awarded*

• *if an indirect free kick is kicked directly into the team's own goal, after the ball is in play, a corner kick is awarded to the opposing team*

Position of Free Kick

Free kick inside the penalty area

Direct or indirect free kick to the defending team:

• *all opponents are at least 9.15 m (10 yds) from the ball*

• *all opponents remain outside the penalty area until the ball is in play*

• *the ball is in play when it is kicked directly beyond the penalty area*

• *a free kick awarded in the goal area is taken from any point inside that area*

Indirect free kick to the attacking team:

• *all opponents are at least 9.15 m (10 yds) from the ball until it is in play, unless they are on their own goal line between the goalposts*

• *the ball is in play when it is kicked and moves*

• *an indirect free kick awarded inside the goal area is taken from that part of the goal area line which runs parallel*

to the goal line, at the point nearest to where the infringement occurred

Free kick outside the penalty area

• *all opponents are at least 9.15 m (10 yds) from the ball until it is in play*

• *the ball is in play when it is kicked and moves*

• *the free kick is taken from where the infringement occurred*

Infringements/Sanctions

If, when a free kick is taken, an opponent is closer to the ball than the required distance:

• *the kick is retaken*

If, when a free kick is taken by the defending team from inside its own penalty area, the ball is not kicked directly into play:

• *the kick is retaken*

Free kick taken by a player other than the goalkeeper

If, after the ball is in play, the kicker touches the ball a second time (except with his hands) before it has touched another player:

• *an indirect free kick is awarded to the opposing team, the kick to be taken from the place where the infringement occurred* [see page 110]

If, after the ball is in play, the kicker deliberately handles the ball before it has touched another player:

• *a direct free kick is awarded to the opposing team, the kick to be taken from the place where the infringement occurred* [see page 110]

• *a penalty kick is awarded if the infringement occurred inside the kicker's penalty area*

Free kick taken by the goalkeeper

If, after the ball is in play, the goalkeeper touches the ball a second time (except with his hands), before it has touched another player:

• *an indirect free kick is awarded to the opposing team, the kick to be taken from the place where the infringement occurred** [see page 110]

If, after the ball is in play, the goalkeeper deliberately handles the ball before it has touched another player:

• *a direct free kick is awarded to the opposing team if the infringement occurred outside the goalkeeper's penalty area, the kick to be taken from the place where the infringement occurred** [see page 110]

• *an indirect free kick is awarded to the opposing team if the infringement occurred inside the goalkeeper's penalty area, the kick to be taken from the place where the infringement occurred** [see page 110]

LAW 14 – The Penalty Kick

A penalty kick is awarded against a team which commits one of the ten offences for which a direct free kick is awarded, inside its own penalty area and while the ball is in play.

A goal may be scored directly from a penalty kick.

Additional time is allowed for a penalty kick to be taken at the end of each half or at the end of periods of extra time.

Position of the Ball and the Players

The ball:

• *is placed on the penalty mark*

The player taking the penalty kick:

• *is properly identified*

The defending goalkeeper:

• *remains on his goal line, facing the kicker, between the goalposts until the ball has been kicked*

The players other than the kicker are located:

• *inside the field of play*

• *outside the penalty area*

• *behind the penalty mark*

• *at least 9.15 m (10 yds) from the penalty mark*

The Referee

• *does not signal for a penalty kick to be taken until the players have taken up position in accordance with the Law*

• *decides when a penalty kick has been completed*

Procedure

• *the player taking the penalty kicks the ball forward*

• *he does not play the ball a second time until it has touched another player*

• *the ball is in play when it is kicked and moves forward*

When a penalty kick is taken during the normal course of play, or time has been extended at half time or full time to allow a penalty kick to be taken or retaken, a goal is awarded if, before passing between the goalposts and under the crossbar:

• *the ball touches either or both of the goalposts and/or the crossbar, and/or the goalkeeper*

Infringements/Sanctions

If the referee gives the signal for a penalty kick to be taken and, before the ball is in play, one of the following situations occurs:

Laws of the Game

The player taking the penalty kick infringes the Laws of the Game:

- *the referee allows the kick to proceed*

- *if the ball enters the goal, the kick is retaken*

- *if the ball does not enter the goal, the kick is not retaken*

The goalkeeper infringes the Laws of the Game:

- *the referee allows the kick to proceed*

- *if the ball enters the goal, a goal is awarded*

- *if the ball does not enter the goal, the kick is retaken*

A team mate of the player taking the kick enters the penalty area or moves in front of or within 9.15 m (10 yds) of the penalty mark:

- *the referee allows the kick to proceed*

- *if the ball enters the goal, the kick is retaken*

- *if the ball does not enter the goal, the kick is not retaken*

- *if the ball rebounds from the goal-keeper, the crossbar or the goal post and is touched by this player, the referee stops play and restarts the match with an indirect free kick to the defending team*

A team mate of the goalkeeper enters the penalty area or moves in front of or within 9.15 m (10 yds) of the penalty mark:

- *the referee allows the kick to proceed*

- *if the ball enters the goal, a goal is awarded*

- *if the ball does not enter the goal, the kick is retaken*

A player of both the defending team and the attacking team infringe the Laws of the Game:

- *the kick is retaken*

If, after the penalty kick has been taken:

The kicker touches the ball a second time (except with his hands) before it has touched another player:

- *an indirect free kick is awarded to the opposing team, the kick to be taken from the place where the infringement occurred* [see page 110]*

The kicker deliberately handles the ball before it has touched another player:

- *a direct free kick is awarded to the opposing team, the kick to be taken from the place where the infringement occurred* [see page 110]*

The ball is touched by an outside agent as it moves forward:

- *the kick is retaken*

The ball rebounds into the field of play from the goalkeeper, the crossbar or the goalposts, and is then touched by an outside agent:

- *the referee stops play*

- *play is restarted with a dropped ball at the place where it touched the out-side agent* [see page 110]*

LAW 15 – The Throw-In

A throw-in is a method of restarting play.

A goal cannot be scored directly from a throw-in.

A throw-in is awarded:

- *when the whole of the ball passes over the touch line, either on the ground or in the air*

• *from the point where it crossed the touch line*

• *to the opponents of the player who last touched the ball*

Procedure
At the moment of delivering the ball, the thrower:

• *faces the field of play*

• *has part of each foot either on the touch line or on the ground outside the touch line*

• *uses both hands*

• *delivers the ball from behind and over his head*

The thrower may not touch the ball again until it has touched another player.

The ball is in play immediately it enters the field of play.

Infringements/Sanctions

Throw-in taken by a player other than the goalkeeper

If, after the ball is in play, the thrower touches the ball a second time (except with his hands) before it has touched another player:

• *an indirect free kick is awarded to the opposing team, the kick to be taken from the place where the infringement occurred* [see page 110]

If, after the ball is in play, the thrower deliberately handles the ball before it has touched another player:

• *a direct free kick is awarded to the opposing team, the kick to be taken from the place where the infringement occurred* [see page 110]

• *a penalty kick is awarded if the infringement occurred inside the thrower's penalty area*

Throw-in taken by the goalkeeper

If, after the ball is in play, the goalkeeper touches the ball a second time (except with his hands), before it has touched another player:

• *an indirect free kick is awarded to the opposing team, the kick to be taken from the place where the infringement occurred* [see page 110]

If, after the ball is in play, the goalkeeper deliberately handles the ball before it has touched another player:

• *a direct free kick is awarded to the opposing team if the infringement occurred outside the goalkeeper's penalty area, the kick to be taken from the place where the infringement occurred* [see page 110]

• *an indirect free kick is awarded to the opposing team if the infringement occurred inside the goalkeeper's penalty area, the kick to be taken from the place where the infringement occurred* [see page 110]

If an opponent unfairly distracts or impedes the thrower:

• *he is cautioned for unsporting behaviour and shown the yellow card*

For any other infringement of this Law:

• *the throw-in is taken by a player of the opposing team*

Laws of the Game

LAW 16 – The Goal Kick

A goal kick is a method of restarting play.

A goal may be scored directly from a goal kick, but only against the opposing team.

A goal kick is awarded when:

• *the whole of the ball, having last touched a player of the attacking team, passes over the goal line, either on the ground or in the air, and a goal is not scored in accordance with Law 10*

Procedure

• *the ball is kicked from any point within the goal area by a player of the defending team*

• *opponents remain outside the penalty area until the ball is in play*

• *the kicker does not play the ball a second time until it has touched another player*

• *the ball is in play when it is kicked directly beyond the penalty area*

Infringements/Sanctions

If the ball is not kicked directly into play beyond the penalty area:

• *the kick is retaken*

Goal kick taken by a player other than the goalkeeper

If, after the ball is in play, the kicker touches the ball a second time (except with his hands) before it has touched another player:

• *an indirect free kick is awarded to the opposing team, the kick to be taken from the place where the infringement occurred* [see page 110]*

If, after the ball is in play, the kicker deliberately handles the ball before it has touched another player:

• *a direct free kick is awarded to the opposing team, the kick to be taken from the place where the infringement occurred* [see page 110]*

• *a penalty kick is awarded if the infringement occurred inside the kicker's penalty area*

Goal kick taken by the goalkeeper

If, after the ball is in play, the goalkeeper touches the ball a second time (except with his hands) before it has touched another player:

• *an indirect free kick is awarded to the opposing team, the kick to be taken from the place where the infringement occurred* [see page 110]*

If, after the ball is in play, the goalkeeper deliberately handles the ball before it has touched another player:

• *a direct free kick is awarded to the opposing team if the infringement occurred outside the goalkeeper's penalty area, the kick to be taken from the place where the infringement occurred* [see page 110]*

• *an indirect free kick is awarded to the opposing team if the infringement occurred inside the goalkeeper's penalty area, the kick to be taken from the place where the infringement occurred* [see page 110]*

For any other infringements of this Law:

• *the kick is retaken*

Laws of the Game

LAW 17 – The Corner Kick

A corner kick is a method of restarting play.

A goal may be scored directly from a corner kick, but only against the opposing team.

A corner kick is awarded when:

• *the whole of the ball, having last touched a player of the defending team, passes over the goal line, either on the ground or in the air, and a goal is not scored in accordance with Law 10*

Procedure

• *the ball is placed inside the corner arc at the nearest corner flagpost*

• *the corner flagpost is not moved*

• *opponents remain at least 9.15 m (10 yds) from the ball until it is in play*

• *the ball is kicked by a player of the attacking team*

• *the ball is in play when it is kicked and moves*

• *the kicker does not play the ball a second time until it has touched another player*

Infringements/Sanctions

Corner kick taken by a player other than the goalkeeper

If, after the ball is in play, the kicker touches the ball a second time (except with his hands) before it has touched another player:

• *an indirect free kick is awarded to the opposing team, the kick to be taken from the place where the infringement occurred* [see page 110]*

If, after the ball is in play, the kicker deliberately handles the ball before it has touched another player:

• *a direct free kick is awarded to the opposing team, the kick to be taken from the place where the infringement occurred* [see page 110]*

• *a penalty kick is awarded if the infringement occurred inside the kicker's penalty area*

Corner kick taken by the goalkeeper

If, after the ball is in play, the goalkeeper touches the ball a second time (except with his hands) before it has touched another player:

• *an indirect free kick is awarded to the opposing team, the kick to be taken from the place where the infringement occurred* [see page 110]*

If, after the ball is in play, the goalkeeper deliberately handles the ball before it has touched another player:

• *a direct free kick is awarded to the opposing team if the infringement occurred outside the goalkeeper's penalty area, the kick to be taken from the place where the infringement occurred* [see page 110]*

• *an indirect free kick is awarded to the opposing team if the infringement occurred inside the goalkeeper's penalty area, the kick to be taken from the place where the infringement occurred* [see page 110]*

For any other infringement:

• *the kick is retaken*

Laws of the Game

Kicks from the Penalty Mark

Taking kicks from the penalty mark is a method of determining the winning team where competition rules require there to be a winning team after a match has been drawn.

Procedure

• When a team finishes the match with a greater number of players than their opponents, they shall reduce their numbers to equate with that of their opponents and inform the referee of the name and number of each player excluded. The team captain has this responsibility.

• Before the start of kicks from the penalty mark the referee shall ensure that only an equal number of players from each team remain within the centre circle and they shall take the kicks.

• The referee chooses the goal at which the kicks will be taken.

• The referee tosses a coin and the team whose captain wins the toss takes the first kick.

• The referee keeps a record of the kicks being taken.

• Subject to the conditions explained below, both teams take five kicks.

• The kicks are taken alternately by the teams.

• If, before both teams have taken five kicks, one has scored more goals than the other could score, even if it were to complete its five kicks, no more kicks are taken.

• If, after both teams have taken five kicks, both have scored the same number of goals, or have not scored any goals, kicks continue to be taken in the same order until one team has scored a goal more than the other from the same number of kicks.

• A goalkeeper who is injured during the taking of kicks from the penalty mark and is unable to continue as goalkeeper may be replaced by a named substitute provided his team has not used the maximum number of substitutes permitted under the competition rules.

• With the exception of the foregoing case, only players who are on the field of play at the end of the match, which includes extra time where appropriate, are allowed to take kicks from the penalty mark.

• Each kick is taken by a different player and all eligible players must take a kick before any player can take a second kick.

• An eligible player may change places with the goalkeeper at any time when kicks from the penalty mark are being taken.

• All players, except the player taking the kick and the two goalkeepers, must remain within the centre circle.

• The goalkeeper who is the team mate of the kicker must remain on the field of play, outside the penalty area in which the kicks are being taken, on the goal line where it meets the penalty area boundary line.

• The other goalkeeper must remain on his goal line between the goalposts, facing the kicker until the ball is kicked.

• Unless otherwise stated, the relevant Laws of the Game and International F.A. Board Decisions apply when kicks from the penalty mark are being taken.

Laws of the Game

The Technical Area

The technical area described in Law 3, International F.A. Board Decision 2, relates particularly to matches played in stadia with a designated seated area for technical staff and substitutes as shown below.

Technical areas may vary between stadia, for example in size or location, and the following notes are issued for general guidance.

• *The technical area extends 1 m (1 yd) on either side of the designated seated area and extends forward up to a distance of 1 m (1 yd) from the touch line.*

• *It is recommended that markings are used to define this area.*

• *The number of persons permitted to occupy the technical area is defined by the competition rules.*

• *The occupants of the technical area are identified before the beginning of the match in accordance with the competition rules.*

• *Only one person at a time is authorised to convey tactical instructions and he must return to his position immediately after giving these instructions.*

• *The coach and other officials must remain within the confines of the technical area except in special circumstances, for example, a physiotherapist or doctor entering the field of play, with the referee's permission, to assess an injured player.*

• *The coach and other occupants of the technical area must behave in a responsible manner.*

The Fourth Official

• *The fourth official may be appointed under the competition rules and officiates if any of the three match officials is unable to continue.*

• *Prior to the start of the competition, the organiser states clearly whether, if the referee is unable to continue, the fourth official takes over as the match referee or whether the senior assistant referee takes over as referee with the fourth official becoming an assistant referee.*

• *The fourth official assists with any administrative duties before, during and after the match, as required by the referee.*

• *He is responsible for assisting with substitution procedures during the match.*

• *He supervises the replacement footballs, where required. If the match ball has to be replaced during a match, he provides another ball, on the instruction of the referee, thus keeping the delay to a minimum.*

• *He has the authority to check the equipment of substitutes before they enter the field of play. If their equipment does not comply with the Laws of the Game, he informs the referee.*

• *He has the authority to inform the referee of irresponsible behaviour by any occupant of the technical area.*

• *The Fourth Official assists the referee at all times. He must indicate to the referee when the wrong player is cautioned because of mistaken identity or when a player is not sent off having been seen to be given a second caution or when violent conduct occurs out of view of the referee and assistant* refeees. The referee, however, retains the authority to decide on all points connected with play.

• After the match, the fourth official must submit a report to the appropriate authorities on any misconduct or other incident which has occurred out of the view of the referee and the assistant referees. The fourth official must advise the referee and his assistants of any report being made.

APPENDIX 1
Assessment

In order to move up through the grades as a referee, it is necessary for the referee to be assessed by a qualified assessor from time to time. In Great Britain, referees start at Class Three on passing the exam in the Laws of the Game. On this grade, referees normally referee in local junior soccer, the lowest level of adult soccer. Promotion to Class Two entitles the referee to referee at a slightly higher level, but is still limited to local and largely amateur soccer. A Class Two promotion normally takes a minimum of two years, with some County Football Associations insisting on a certain number of games before a referee is considered for the move upwards. Promotion to Class One takes at least another year or two, and at this grade, the referee can be considered for a move to a supply league. This represents the first step on the promotional ladder for qualifying as a referee in senior professional football.

Since promotion is gained on a combination of club marks and assessor's marks, the assessor's role is important in career progression. In recent years the FA in Great Britain has put a great deal of importance on the standard of assessments. This has meant that assessors are now thoroughly trained and their training must be updated on a regular basis. This is intended to improve the support given to referees throughout their career, and is being complemented by the development of mentoring schemes and 'Schools of Excellence', whose introduction is now gathering pace. If you have the opportunity to participate in these, it is strongly advised that you do so. While a lot of assessments are concerned with referee promotion, they are increasingly used to provide more advice and support for the referee at every level, and especially in the early part of his career. Assessors are trained to be supportive and sympathetic to the referee. They are not there to point out the faults and weaknesses of a referee, but to give positive support and advice. Occasionally, the local Referees' Association or Football Association will run a course in assessment or a talk or seminar led by an assessor. It is advisable for you to attend these if you possibly can, so you can pick up more information and a better understanding of the process.

It is useful to consider the marking criteria the assessor uses, and this is set out in the table below.

Performance	Mark-by-mark breakdown and comment		
	Guide comment	Description	Mark
Obviously very superior	A faultless performance.	Excellent	10
	First-class match control from a correct use of authority with only a minor deficiency in one of the other sub-sections.	Outstanding	9
Above average	Worthy of consideration for promotion on this performance (would appear to be capable of handling more demanding matches).	Very good	8
	Above average but not yet recommended for promotion.	Good	7
Average	Only just above average.	Adequate	6
	As competent as expected for this classification (or this senior competition).	Fair	5
Below average	Lacking in match control.	Weak	4
	Severely lacking in match control.	Very weak	3
Unsatisfactory	No match control and below the standard expected in most sub-sections.	Poor	2
	Unacceptably low standard, should be reclassified into a lower grade (or removed from the list of officials on the competition).	Very poor	1

From: *Guide to Marking for Referee Assessors*, The Football Association

Assessment

A referee's first assessment will probably happen in the first few weeks of his refereeing career. This will be an advisory assessment to help the referee gain confidence and to give some constructive advice concerning his performance. Later in his career, assessment will be used to judge whether he should proceed to a higher level. When this occurs, he will experience three, and sometimes four assessments in a season, all from different assessors. These are considered in addition to an average of his season's club marks as the basis for promotion.

It is useful to read the Guide to Assessors (shown below) published by the Football Association, which shows the areas that the referee will be assessed on, and that are important for the referee to address.

Guide to Assessors

1 Appearance
Did he look clean and well turned out?
Did he enter the field confidently?
Were his first impressions good?

2 Signals
Were his decisions clearly indicated by his signals?
Did he make best use of the whistle?
Were his hand signals clear and definite?
Did he indicate indirect free kicks correctly?
Was he too demonstrative in any manner?

3 Stoppages
Did he give decisions promptly and firmly or did he appear doubtful and/or hesitant?
Did he endeavour to get play started as quickly as possible?
Were his attitude and action correct in respect of players who delayed the taking of free kicks, etc.?
Did he act correctly in relation to injuries, etc. by preventing unnecessary stopppages or delays?
Was the correct time allowed for stoppages and time wasting?
Was his estimation of 10 yards reasonable?

4 Advantage
Was the approved signal used consistently?
Did he make too much or too little use of the advantage clause?
If he allowed advantage did he appear to speak or take action against the offender?

Did the players appear to acknowledge or accept the fact that he had played the advantage?

Did he make excessive use of the advantage clause (particularly with respect to contact fouls) with consequent danger of retaliation by players?

If an advantage did not accrue, did he stop the game within a reasonable time and penalise the original offence?

5 Co-operation with Assistant Referees

Did he make effective use of his assistant referees?

Did he allow assistant referees to influence his decisions?

Did he acknowledge signals given by the assistant referees as and when necessary or automatically?

If consultation was necessary did he approach the assistant referees before indicating his decision?

6 Application of the Laws

(a) Penal Offences

   Did he appear to recognise the actions of the players correctly?

   Did he apply the Law correctly?

(b) Technical Offences

   Were his decisions and action on technical offences correct?

(c) Misconduct

   Did he assert his authority firmly without being officious?

   Did he look for trouble?

   How did the players react?

   Were all the incidents dealt with as quickly as possible?

   Did it appear as if he had stopped any trouble at the first attempt?

   Did he allow players to crowd him or permit questioning of his decisions?

7 Positioning and Movement

Did he appear to anticipate play and position himself accordingly?

Did he make use of a 'diagonal system' or merely move up and down the centre?

Did he position himself to the best advantage and well enough to see incidents of a 'set nature' clearly, e.g. corner kicks, goal kicks, etc. and did he allow himself sufficient scope to view possible offences, e.g. pushing, impeding an opponent, etc.?

Did he attempt to keep the assistant referees in view at all times or when it mattered?

Did he keep the centre of the incident in view after awarding a free kick?

Did he follow through for goal line incidents when necessary?

Did he turn his back on play at free kicks, goal kicks, etc.?
Did he get mixed up in the centre of play unnecessarily?
Did he pace himself reasonably well throughout the game?
Was he in position when it really mattered?
Was he at all times quick off the mark?
Could he, and did he, accelerate when the situation demanded it?

8 Control and Authority

Did he appear confidently at ease throughout the match?
Did he inspire respect?
Did he overlook or shirk major issues or decisions?
Was he fussy about trivialities?
Was he a showman?
Did he have any distracting or annoying mannerisms?
Did he use common sense/initiative?
If he lost control can you pinpoint the incident which led to this?
Was there an incident, which led to a loss of player control or,
conversely, turned the control of the game in the referee's favour?

9 General Remarks and Constructive Advice

Was it a particularly difficult match to control?
Did the weather or ground conditions make it difficult?
Were the players co-operative in accepting decisions?
What further advice can you give to the referee that has not already
been covered by sections 1–8?

From: *Guide to Assessors*, The Football Association

The above guide shows the structure the assessor will follow when watching the referee, and gives you some idea of the range of factors which the assessor takes into account. It forms an excellent framework for the referee to follow when undertaking his *own* assessment of his performance after the game. The assessor should not just point out where the referee needs advice to improve his game, but also the features of his game which are strong.

Below is a copy of a completed FA assessment form illustrating how the marking and guidelines work in practice.

Referee Assessment Form

Name of Referee: John Thompson
Match: Red Lion v Newtown   **Date:** 9th September 2000
League/Competition: Junior Cup
State of Ground: Soft, grassy, long and damp. Indistinct pitch markings
Weather Conditions: Cool, very blustery
Were the linesmen Neutral or Club officials?
Neutral: ....   Club: Club assistant referees were used

1. Appearance: Your appearance was professional and tidy. You inspected the field 35 minutes before the start of play and briefed both assistant referees.

2. Signals: You used the whistle well. Arm signals for offside and throw-ins, goal-kicks and corners were clear and distinct. You used your voice well to advise players of your decisions.

3. Stoppages: You dealt with stoppages for injury correctly and promptly, and added time on accurately.

4. Advantage: You tried to keep the game flowing, and particularly played the advantage well when receiving signals for offside from the assistant referees, which you rightly over-ruled. This was also communicated well both to players and the assistant referees. On one occasion in the first half, you gave an advantage after a rather heavy challenge by the Red Lion No. 6. This could have resulted in retaliation, and you dealt with the subsequent argument between the players well. I understand the speed with which you have to make such a decision but please be aware of the danger of playing the advantage where there is a strong possibility of the situation getting out of hand.

5. Co-operation with Assistant Referees: You generally acknowledged the assistant referees well, including when you decided to over-rule them, and this was a positive point in your game.

6. Application of the Laws: Your application of the Laws was accurate.

7. Positioning and Movement: Your use of the diagonal was good. You kept your eye on play, and tried to anticipate the movement of the game. This was not always easy given the very windy conditions.

You always faced play to keep a clear view of the game. Your position at corners was very good, occasionally going close to the goal-line to get as good a view as necessary. The nature of the game was such that you did not neeed to sprint into position too often, and you always seemed to be in the right position when it mattered.

In the early stages of the game, you seemed to have difficulty in assessing the dropping zone when the ball was being kicked into play by the goalkeeper, and this made for some slight difficulty in the confrontation between the centre-forward and centre-half. Consider standing more wide in this situation.

8. Overall Control and Authority: I thought that your overall control was very good. You maintained control in a quiet and firm way. You rightly cautioned a Red Lion player in the 30th minute of the first half for a late challenge on the opposition goalkeeper. I thought that your cautioning of the Newtown No. 10 near the end of the first half was well merited. This caution had some effect on the game, and made your job easier after the break. Please think about cautioning such players a little earlier as this was his sixth foul in 15 minutes. I feel that you would have been within your rights to take action earlier had you wished.

9. General Remarks and Constructive Advice: I think that this was a very creditable performance. You tried wherever possible to keep the game flowing and you retained control throughout. Although the game appeared to be easy to control, I think that this was because you worked hard to make it so. Your strengths included good positioning, a good rapport with the players and a firm and confident manner. Please consider the following points: use of advantage following a heavy challenge; issuing an earlier caution when a player has committed several unfair challenges; positioning in the centre of the field to keep a clear view of the dropping zone.

Date: 10th September 2000   Signature of Assessor: ....

Name in Block Capitals: ....

Assessment

Dos and don'ts

1 If you think, or know that you are being assessed, play your normal game and do not try to play a different game for the assessor.

2 Always look carefully at your assessment report. It has been written with the intention of helping you to develop your game.

3 Don't try to tackle the assessor at the end of the game. Assessors are told to avoid speaking to the referee at the end of the game. Often it is better to talk to the assessor at a later stage, sometime after the game when you and he have both had a chance to think the game through.

4 You should certainly not approach the referee for advice or comment at half-time.

5 The assessor will be appointed to your game a few days beforehand. If, for any reason, you are unable to referee a game, you should ring the Referees' Secretary, or whoever is responsible for allocating assessors to games, and let him know. This will avoid wasting an assessor's time.

6 Don't ask the assessor for the mark he has awarded. This is confidential.

Assessment is intended to be a valuable and helpful experience for you and you should try to gain as much benefit from it as you can.

APPENDIX 2
Notes on Diet and Fitness

Taking a positive attitude to diet and fitness will help you succeed as a referee. It is now possible to get a great deal of good advice from fitness experts, or from visiting a local leisure centre or gym. This chapter is designed to give an overview of the essential dos and don'ts for the referee.

It is not so many years ago that players were given steak before a game. The biography of a number of leading players shows a predilection for consuming beer in large quantities after a game, often while still dehydrated, and sometimes not long before a key game as well. A former colleague of mine, who had played County level rugby in his younger days, once told me that in his day, training consisted mostly of beer and cigarettes! It is only in recent years that the attitude towards diet and fitness among sportsmen has become much more scientific and professional.

The game has, in recent years, become much faster and more athletic. Even at a local level, players are likely to be fitter and faster. Not so many years ago, a non-league side of part-time players taking on a professional team were likely to tire in the last part of the game, as the full-time professional players were fitter and better trained. The development of better facilities and more rigorous methods of training have changed this, and now even part-time soccer players can achieve the same level of fitness as full-time professionals.

The greater speed and athleticism of the game has in turn put pressure on referees to become more professional in their approach to fitness and diet. The physical demands of the game for a referee can be summarised as follows:

- In an average game the referee will cover 6–8 miles.
- The majority of this distance will be covered by jogging or walking at a gentle pace.
- About 1000–2000 yards will be covered by sprinting at three-quarter speed or faster.

Diet

To perform well, a referee must be able to meet the physical demands of the game. His diet must include an adequate intake of food to produce a suitable amount of 'fuel'. The important thing is to achieve the right amount: he must have enough food to give him sufficient energy to referee competently, but not too much that he becomes overweight and his performance deteriorates. For more detailed information concerning diet, I recommend consulting a dietician or sports nutritionist. The following is a brief guide to the essential dos and don'ts:

Dos and don'ts

1 Do organise your eating. It is important to refuel, so fit your eating around training. Don't eat immediately before training, but eat a reasonable meal and allow enough time for it to digest.

2 Do eat a good quantity of cereals, which are high in carbohydrates, including wholemeal bread, wholegrain breakfast cereal or porridge, pasta, noodles, rice and potatoes.

3 Have a good breakfast including porridge, wholegrain cereal or bread and baked beans, plus fruit juice and tea or coffee.

4 Do try reduce your consumption of fats. This includes not only the more obvious *visible* fats, such as butter, oils or fat on meat, but also *invisible* fats which are found in milk, dairy produce, eggs (eat no more than five per week), sausages, pies, burgers and nuts. Try to grill rather than fry food.

5 Do try to reduce your consumption of red meats, such as beef, pork and lamb. It is advisable to eat them once a week only. Replace these with white meats, such as chicken and turkey.

6 Don't smoke!

7 If you drink alcohol, do so in moderation.

8 Do reduce your consumption of salt and food high in salt, such as pickled and smoked foods.

9 Don't eat a lot of sugary foods.

10 Eat plenty of fruit and vegetables.

On the day of a match itself, try the following diet:

- Breakfast high in carbohydrates, e.g. a high-fibre cereal or porridge, two thick slices of wholemeal toast, fruit juice and a piece of fresh fruit.
- A drink of water or fruit juice and a banana mid-morning.
- Undertake a light training session to raise blood sugar levels.
- Take a meal high in carbohydrates about three hours before the start of the game, such as pasta, rice, or a jacket potato.

Try to eat after the game, when your body will need refuelling. In my experience, the release of tension after the game always gave me a healthy appetite and I was quick to find some suitable sustenance.

Finally, remember to take plenty of fluids. Fresh fruit juice or water is important to ensure that you are not dehydrated. If dehydration does occur and you become thirsty, it is already too late. It is worth remembering that for every one per cent loss in body weight through dehydration, performance deteriorates by 10 per cent. Your last drink before a game should be taken not less than 30 minutes before kick-off, so that it is fully absorbed into the body and has left the stomach. It is advisable to avoid drinking diuretic drinks three to six hours before the kick off. These include tea, coffee, alcohol, chocolate, milks and colas.

You should plan a good dietary regime that is useful for *all* of the year and not just for the day of the match. This regime should form part of a lifestyle to ensure long-term good health and good performance on the field.

Fitness and training

Fitness is very important to the successful referee. Not only does it enable the referee to keep up with play and thus make accurate decisions, but it also enables him to avoid fatigue. Fatigue reduces concentration and increases the risk of making errors.

To meet the physical demands of the game a referee needs cardiovascular fitness and local muscle endurance. Cardiovascular fitness is generated by the heart, lungs and circulatory system; local muscle endurance enables particular groups of muscles to function effectively over a long period of time. Another way of looking at this is to summarise the physical activity of a referee as comprising acceleration, speed, manoeuvrability, and stamina.

In assessing referees I am often disappointed at the lack of fitness of even quite young referees. This shows in a number of ways, such as an inability to get close to the action when an attacking breakaway occurs. There is also a problem in using the whole diagonal. This all works against the referee in trying to gain control of the game. Lack of fitness means that you are unlikely to be able to see a situation properly, and thus fail to retain control of the game and win the respect of the players. Players will respect a referee's decision more if the referee is up with play and not a long way out of position.

Easy ways of improving fitness include leisure and sports centres, gyms, squash clubs, etc. Many gyms or sports centres offer circuit training, which is especially useful for general fitness training. A further possibility for the referee is to take advantage of training offered by a soccer club, and to train with the players. This might also be useful in building up links with players and officials which will aid understanding and awareness. In my experience it is always better to train with other people in an organised way. This gives you a disciplined framework in which to work, and ensures that you complete the training properly. There are also a number of sports that help to develop both physical fitness and mental alertness such as squash, tennis, basketball, and volleyball. These sports enable the participant to gain skills in observing, assessing a situation, speedy decision-making and appropriate physical action.

Detailed training programmes should be obtained from professional organisations as outlined above. The information included below provides some general advice for referees on developing a positive and useful approach to training and fitness.

It is very important to maintain a consistent approach to training. Ideally you should train three to five times a week – including at least 20 minutes of aerobic exercise. (Aerobic exercise is where your pulse rate is 60–85% of your maximum heart rate. Your maximum heart rate is found by deducting your age from 220.) If you train with a professional organisation your training should be properly handled and managed. If you are undertaking your own training, try to follow the advice given below.

First, it is important to warm up for about 10–15 minutes. Start by alternately jogging and walking – 50 yards of each for 2–3 minutes and then 100 yards of each. After this, undertake stretching and mobilising activities for about 10 minutes. These exercises are aimed at stretching and stimulating the muscles in preparation for heavier exercise, and to ensure that strains and injuries do not occur. There are many ways of doing this, but yhou should try to ensure that all muscles are well stretched and thus ready for heavy exercise.

You can now undertake some speed and endurance work. This can be varied, and if you look in some specialist textbooks, you will find a range of different programmes to follow. It is useful to vary your training to include a mixture of walking, jogging and sprinting to build up stamina and speed. One type of programme for speed work is known as 'fartlek', a Swedish term meaning 'speed play'. It involves continuous activity for at least 20 minutes, varying in speed from walking, jogging, medium-pace running and sprinting. This, of course, reflects what actually happens to a referee in a game. A programme of interval training, like 'fartlek', which involves a series of short sprints, longer distances at medium speed and short rests in between is valuable.

A sample interval programme is listed below, which is especially useful if you live in an urban environment. It involves the use of lampposts to judge the interval in which you can vary your exercise.

- Jog at an easy pace for three lampposts.
- Sprint to the next lamppost.
- Jog at an easy pace for three lampposts.
- Sprint to the next lamppost.
- Repeat this process three more times.
- Walk for one minute.
- Jog at 75% of maximum heart rate for a further five minutes.

Remember that at the end of the training session you should 'cool down', which involves taking light exercise during the recovery period. The purpose of this is to help flush out waste products from the body, such as lactic acid and carbon dioxide, and thus reduce recovery time. It is also important for distributing blood to the working muscles. If muscle action stops suddenly, the amount of blood returning to the heart also stops dramatically, and light-headedness and dizziness can result due to the swift drop in blood pressure. Furthermore, if muscles cool down very suddenly they can be damaged. The cool down allows physical and mental relaxation, swifter recovery and avoids injury and muscle soreness.

Dos and don'ts

1 Do make an effort to build up your fitness by regular exercise.

2 Don't let yourself make excuses to avoid a regular session.

3 Do try to work with other people as much as possible, so that you can motivate each other to train properly.

Notes on Diet and Fitness

4 Do try to take up another sport if you haven't already. This means that the skills of judging situations at speed, co-ordination of movement and speed of reaction can be developed, as well as physical fitness.

5 Don't overdo things if you are not very fit. It is better to build up gradually.

6 Don't train if you are feeling unwell.

7 Don't undertake heavy training the day before you referee.

8 Do make sure that you warm up immediately before the game.

9 Do things which are not only helpful in raising your fitness, but which you also find enjoyable and fun to do.

10 Keep a record of what you do to help in ensuring progression and maintaining motivation.

Finally, remember that it takes a long time to develop fitness, but only a third of that time to lose it! Thus, it is important to have a regular training schedule and to stick to it.

Useful addresses

Fédération Internationale de
Football Association (FIFA)
FIFA House
Hitzigweg 11
PO Box 85
8030 Zürich
Switzerland
Tel: (41-1) 384 95 95
Fax: (41-1) 384 96 96
Website: www.fifa.com

UEFA
46 Geneva Road
1260 Nuon 2
Switzerland
Tel: (41-22) 994 44 44
Fax: (41-22) 994 44 88
Website: www.uefa.com

The Football Association
Refereeing Department
16 Lancaster Gate
London W2 3LW
Tel: (020) 7402 7151 and
(020) 7262 4542
Fax: (020) 7402 0486
Website: www.the-fa.org

The Referees' Association
1 Westhill Road
Coundon
Coventry
West Midlands CV6 2AD
Tel: (01203) 601701
Fax: (01203) 601556
Website: www.referee.u-k.org

United States Soccer Federation
1801 South Prairie Avenue
Chicago, IL 60616
Tel: (312) 808 1300
Fax: (312) 808 1301
Website: www.us-soccer.com
E-mail: socfed@aol.com

U.S. Youth Soccer Association
899 Presidential Drive, Suite 117
Richardson, TX 75081
Tel: 1-800-4SOCCER
Fax: (972) 235 4480
Website: www.usysa.com

American Youth Soccer
Organization
12501 South Isis Avenue
Hawthorne, CA 90250
Tel: 1-800-USA-AYSO
Fax: (310) 643 5310
Website: www.aysa.com

Index

Entries in **bold** refer to the Laws of the Game section.

abandonment   4, 81–2
advantage, playing the   5–6
assaults   70, 81-2
assessment   135–42
assistant referees   **120**
  briefing   18–20
  club   18–19
  duties of   13–23
  neutral   7, 13, 17–20
  offside law   54–5
  positioning   97–8
  signals of   14–16

ball   2, 33–4, **114**
  in and out of play   45–6, **122**
bleeding   5

cards   11, 79
cautions   6, 73–6, 78–9
coaching from the line   35–6
Cooper Test of physical fitness   9, 25
corner kicks   21–2, 107–8, **130–1**

diagonal system of control   17
diet, notes on   143–5
disciplinary action   6
dissent   71, 73–4
dress   8
dropped ball   44–5

equipment   2, 10–12, 38–9, **116–17**

field of play   26–33, 75–6, **112–13**
  centre circle   28
  corner area   29
  dimensions   26, 30
  goal area   28
  goals   31–2
  markings   27–9
  penalty area   28–9
  safety   32–3
fitness, notes on   145–8
fouls   58–84, **123–5**
fourth official   1, 23, **133**
free kicks   85–90,   **125–7**

goalkeepers   35, 67–9, 93–4
goal kicks   21, 106–7, **129–30**

half-time   42

impartiality   9
impeding   66
injury, stoppages for   4

kick-off   43–5

Laws of the Game   1, 26, 98, **110–34**

misconduct   58–84, **123–5**

non-penal offences   65–9

offside   47–55, **123**

penal offences   6, 58–64
penalty kicks   22–3, 91–100, **127–8**
'penalty shoot-outs'   98–100, **131–2**
play
  duration of   42–3, **120**
  re-start of   7–8, 21–3, 74–5, 88, **121–2**
  start of   43–5, **121–2**
players, number of   35–8, **115–16**
positioning   21–3, 91–8
'professional foul'   69

record, keeping a   2–3
referee   **117–19**
  duties of   1–12
Referee's Association   8, 21, 82
reports, of misconduct   8, 80–1

scoring   3, 47, **122**
sendings-off   6, 73–9
serious foul play   77
substitutes   36–8

team officials   7
'technical' area   7, **132**
throw-ins   102–6, **128–9**
timekeeping   2–3

unauthorised persons   7
unsporting behaviour   70–1, 73

violent conduct   77